The King's Cousins
A History of Clan McGrath

By
Dan McGrath

DanMcGrath.net

PAPERBACK

FIRST EDITION

Published by Dan McGrath in
Minneapolis, Minnesota
United States of America
DanMcGrath.net

Cover Art by Dan McGrath

Library of Congress Control Number: 2025924322

ISBN: 979-8-9876169-4-9

"Salus In Fide"
(Salvation Through Faith)

-The motto of Clan McGrath

Contents

Dedicated to my brothers, Steven and Jason

and

All of my McGrath cousins.

The First McGrath

My given name is Daniel Patrick McGrath Jr. – A mix of Danny Boy, Saint Patrick and a surname indicating I'm a distant cousin to Brian Boru. I'm American by birth and culture, but have strong Irish ancestry on both sides of my family and that ancestry hasn't been forgotten, as you can probably discern from my name. I was always curious about Ireland and my ancestry, but a trip to the Emerald Isle sparked a more vigorous fascination and I wanted to get to the origins of my clan. The prefix "Mc" or "Mac" means "son of" or "descends from" in Gaelic, the same way "son" or "sen" works as a suffix for Scandinavian peoples. So I wanted to know, "Who the heck was was 'Grath?'" – the son of whom presumably gave my family our persistent surname.

What I learned was surprising and exciting. The McGraths have quite a storied history with intimate links to the Kennedys and the O'Briens, starting with Cennétig (Kennedy) and his son Brian Boru.

When most people hear the name Brian Boru, they think of one of Ireland's greatest kings – the First High King of Ireland, the man who rose from a small dynasty in Thomond (situated in Counties Clare and Limerick) to wear the crown uniting the island, later to die quite famously, subduing the Vikings at the Battle of Clontarf in 1014. But Brian wasn't the only notable son of his father, Cennétig mac Lorcáin (whose descendants through

Brian's line also brought about the Clan O'Kennedy, later shortened to Kennedy). Among his brothers were Mathgamain (Mahon) and Echtiern (also spelled Echthigern and Anglicized as Ahern or Aherne), progenitor of the Irish clan that would become known as McGrath. Not kings themselves, but cousins to the O'Brien royal family and direct descendants of King Cennétig of Thomond, the McGraths were crucial in the preservation of Irish culture and history.

It's through Echtiern that Clan McGrath finds its origin, and through him that the McGraths share in the same royal bloodline that produced High King Brian Boru. While Brian's direct line became the O'Briens, kings and rulers of Thomond for centuries, Echtiern's descendants took a different path. They chose not the sword or the throne, but the pen, the memory, and the spirit of Ireland.

To understand the McGraths' place, we should first look back at their royal ancestor. Cennétig mac Lorcáin, king of Thomond lived in the turbulent tenth century when the Vikings were raiding Ireland's coasts and the Irish provincial kings jostled for territory and supremacy. His dynasty, the Dál gCais (Dalcass), was not yet very powerful. In fact, they were seen as upstarts by the mighty Eóganachta of Munster, who had ruled from Cashel for centuries.

But Cennétig's sons changed that balance. His eldest, Mathgamain, seized the kingship of Munster. His younger son, Brian Boru, outdid him, becoming High King of Ireland. And then there was Echtiern, who didn't leave behind the same trail of storied and bloody battles, but whose bloodline carried forward to serve the dynasty and the island in a different way.

Irish surnames were just starting to take form around this period, and they often crystallized not from the founding ancestor himself, but from a memorable descendant a generation or two later. That's exactly what happened in Echtiern's family.

Some generations after Echtiern, appeared a man remembered as Craith. He was either Echtiern's grandson or great-grandson. Unfortunately, even though the proto-McGraths were renowned as historians, the exact generation has been lost to time, as far as I can discern. Recording the mighty deeds of the O'Briens was their focus. The writers evidently didn't often write about themselves.

The name Craith also translated to meanings of grace or prosperity which some may have thought particularly fitting for the clan's continued lineage, given their role in Irish society. In any case, it was short, strong, and easy to hold on the tongue – more so than "Echthigern," which never became a surname in its own right (although Aherne eventually did).

And so Echtiern's descendants finally settled on the name Mac Craith – the Sons of Grace. The name remembers the man, Craith, but also speaks of dignity, divinity and a regal genealogy. The settled clan name may have been the early McGraths' way of saying, "we may not be kings, but we share the royal blood."

From early on, the McGraths distinguished themselves not by seizing crowns or land, but by becoming masters of Ireland's cultural lifeblood: poetry, history, religion and learning. In Gaelic society, this role was anything but minor. The ollamh, the chief poet or historian, was second only to the king in prestige.

By the Twelfth Century, the McGraths had established themselves as the hereditary ollamhs of Thomond, serving their cousins, the O'Briens, who still ruled the province. They composed verse that celebrated victories, they recorded genealogies, and they preserved the stories that gave meaning to and legitimized the O'Briens' rule. Without the McGraths, much of the O'Brien and O'Kennedy legacies might well have slipped into obscurity.

A bardic school (Clann Chraith Bardic School) established by the early McGraths gained renown, producing famous works such as 'The Wars of Thomond' and 'Coin airdfhiadhaigh Clann Choiléin' (The Noble Hounds of the Clan O'Collins).

In an age before printing presses, these bards and poets were keepers of the living memory of a people. Their words could immortalize a lord's glory or cut down an enemy's honor. To be the custodians of such power was no small thing.

Like many prominent Irish families, the McGraths spread into different regions, eventually taking on different roles while still carrying the name forward. All across Ireland, the landscape is punctuated with monuments and ruins associated with Clan McGrath, including at least four castles.

In Thomond (Clare and Limerick), they remained the great learned family of poets and chroniclers to the O'Briens.

In the Decies of Waterford, a southern branch of the clan tied itself closely to the Church, taking guardianship of ecclesiastical lands.

In Ulster, the McGraths became lords of Termonmagrath, near Pettigo in modern Donegal. There, they served as protectors of church territory, blending spiritual responsibility with temporal authority. The partial ruins of Termon Castle McGrath still stand there.

In every branch, a notable pattern seems to repeat: while others fought with steel over gold crowns, the McGraths safeguarded knowledge, faith, and memory and expanded their influence with the power of the pen.

It's striking to see how many great Irish families sprang from Cennétig mac Lorcáin's household. The O'Briens, of course, descended from Brian Boru and held the kingship of Thomond. The O'Kennedys arose from Cennétig's grandson through Brian's line, and became lords of Ormond in Tipperary (and of course, the Kennedys later went on to produce one of the United States' most famous and beloved presidents, John F. Kennedy). And the

McGraths, from Echtiern, became the great historians and poets of the same dynasty. All were branches of the same Dál gCais stock, cousins in blood but distinct in their intertwined destinies.

If the O'Briens were remembered for their crowns, and the O'Kennedys for their lordships, then the McGraths were remembered for their words. The name they chose: Mac Craith, "sons of grace," seems almost prophetic. For centuries, they gave grace to Ireland through learning and poetry, weaving songs and stories that have outlasted swords and fortresses. That's why, even today, the McGraths can claim with pride not just kinship with the first High King Brian Boru, but a legacy uniquely their own: the keepers of memory and teachers of poetry and literature in a land where stories are everything.

Like so many Irish names, Mac Craith did not stand still. As centuries passed and Gaelic Ireland collided with Norman scribes, English administrators, and Anglicization, the spelling bent and shifted. The original Mac Craith was rendered in medieval manuscripts in several ways: Macraith, Mag Raith, M'Grath and others, depending on the scribe's ear and the alphabet at hand. When English rule pressed harder in the sixteenth and seventeenth centuries, the name was simplified again, most often to McGrath. That form became dominant in Munster and Ulster alike, and it remains the most common today.

Other variations, however, are still out there, all pointing back to the same lineage. In some regions, softer pronunciation produced McGraw, a spelling that took root especially among emigrant families in America. Elsewhere you find Macrae, Macraith, M'Graw, and even the Scottish-influenced Magrath. Though they look different on paper, they are all branches of the same trunk, born from Echtiern's line and the memory of his grandson, Craith. In a way, the many spellings are part of the story – each a fossil of how a Gaelic name sounded to foreign ears, and each a reminder of how Irish families carried their identity through English oppression, bureaucracy, shifting languages and migration to new lands.

All one family:

- Mac Craith – the original form.
- McGrath – the most common modern rendition (Anglicized).
- Mac Raith – an early form of the surname.
- Mag Raith – another early variant.
- Macraith – a later rendition.
- Magrath – a variant still in use today.
- McGraw – found in both Ireland and Scotland, particularly in Ulster.
- Macrae / MacRae – common in Scotland, though they may have different Gaelic origins.
- McCraw – another Scottish variant.
- McCreagh – found in certain Irish records.
- MacReagh – a variant with historical usage.
- McCreath – less common but still documented.
- MacGraith – a direct Anglicization.
- MacGrae – a simplified form.
- Makrayth – an archaic variant.
- McKray – a rare form.

Echtiern's Life and Times

Alas, though his decedents, the McGrath's became hereditary scribes, bards and historians, precious little was recorded about Echtiern, himself. As he was not known to be directly involved in glorified battles or conquests, there are scant facts about his life and deeds, but I'll try to extrapolate from what I do know about him, his famous family and the times in which he lived.

The hills of tenth-century Thomond were alive with the restless energy of a family on the rise. Cennétig mac Lorcáin ruled these lands with the cautious ambition of a man who knew the Eóganachta still cast long shadows over Munster. His sons, Mathgamain, Brian, and Echtiern each carried a spark of his drive, but each in very different ways.

Mathgamain, the eldest, was the natural warrior, a man who sharpened his sword as deftly as he did his mind for strategy. Brian, fiery and clever, was always a step beyond, thinking in terms of kingship and the high-stakes chessboard of Irish politics. And then there was Echtiern, perhaps quieter but no less formidable in his own domain. While his brothers plotted alliances and waged battles, Echtiern wove knowledge, memory, spirituality and legacy into the fabric of their family.

The brothers spent their youth in hill forts overlooking the river Shannon, where the wind whipped the mist from the water, the rain fell often, but softly, the hills were a vibrant green and the smell of peat smoke filled the air.

Brian would race to the top of a fort to practice with sword and spear, while Mathgamain drilled the household warriors. Echtiern, however, would more likely sit with scribes and scholars, memorizing the annals, and learning the histories of neighboring clans. His eyes saw patterns that a sword could not parse: the rise and fall of families, the ebb and flow of allegiances, the fragile nature of power.

In a simple timber hall, in a simple ring fort perched on a hill at Cashelmore, sat Echtiern. As the rain fell outside and candles flickered within, he might have recalled the genealogies of the Dál gCais for posterity to a company of students and scribes, quills scratching across parchment.

Outside, the Vikings might raid, neighboring clans might quarrel, but inside the hall, history was being written and remembered. Prayers were said and songs composed.

Despite their differences, the Mac Cennétig brothers' paths were intertwined. When raiders did strike the coast, it was Brian who led men to repel them. When Thomond's loyalties wavered, Mathgamain negotiated with wary clan chiefs and neighboring kings. And when the deeds of the day needed to be recorded – the tales of victory, the honors given to warriors, the laws and agreements binding their people, it was Echtiern whose hand preserved their names and decrees for history.

Family quarrels were probably inevitable. These were ambitious people. Brian may have chafed at Echtiern's seeming inaction, perhaps mocking him for "sitting with books while kingdoms are won."

And Echtiern, in turn, may have quietly reminded Brian that a king forgotten by history is no king at all. "You fight battles today, but without memory, they vanish tomorrow. A sword can cut a man down, but only the stories endure," he might have chided.

In the midst of turbulent tenth-century Ireland, Echtiern was born into a family with ambition in their blood, and even if they didn't always see eye to eye, together, they sculpted Ireland's future.

The winds of Munster carried whispers of conflict and unrest. Mathgamain, the eldest brother, was a man of steel and calculation. He moved through the hills and valleys of Thomond with a warrior's poise, building alliances and quelling rivals. His path to the kingship of Munster was neither easy nor bloodless. He navigated the treacherous politics of the Eóganachta, who had long claimed supremacy in the province, and rallied the Dál gCais clans to his banner. Every skirmish, every clever negotiation, strengthened his growing dominion and every victory brought the family closer to the heights of power that his father had dreamed of.

But Mathgamain's rule, though bold, was overshadowed by the rising brilliance of his younger brother, Brian. Where Mathgamain wielded authority, Brian wielded vision. He saw Munster not as a patchwork of petty kingdoms but as a strategic realm that could unite all of Ireland under one crown. His strategy combined warfare and diplomacy, alliances and cunning – a delicate dance between swords, oaths, and kinship. When Mathgamain was treacherously captured and killed by rivals in 976, the mantle of leadership fell to Brian, who seized the opportunity with both hands. From Thomond's hills to the fertile plains of Munster, he consolidated power, earning the respect (and fear) of friend and foe alike.

By 1002, Brian Boru had risen to the pinnacle of Irish kingship: the High King of Ireland. A king of kings. His influence stretched from the mountains of Ulster to the southern coasts of Munster, from the Viking strongholds in Dublin to the crumbling ringforts of remote clans. And yet, for all his glory, he never forgot the importance of memory. Behind the banners and beside the battlefield, the quieter scribes and poets, Echtiern and his sons chronicled every victory, every oath sworn and broken, every act of valor.

Echtiern, ever the scholar and preserver of history, would have watched these events unfold with a mixture of pride and sober reflection. His pen recorded the rise of his brothers not for glory, but for posterity. Where Brian conquered with sword and will, Echtiern captured with ink and insight. Perhaps he noted the subtle strategies, the loyalty of allies, the rivalries that shaped each battle.

The deeds of Mathgamain and Brian were more than political triumphs. They became stories, lessons, and legends, preserved by the hand of a man whose strength lay not in command, but in memory. And though Echtiern himself never wore a crown, through him, the legacy of the Dál gCais would endure, the rise of kings immortalized and legitimized in the quiet, indelible work of the McGrath line.

Echtiern fathered sons who carried forward the Mac Craith name. From this branch would spring a long lineage of scholars, poets, and church custodians. They were the hereditary ollamhs of Thomond. These men preserved the histories of the O'Briens, chronicled the Wars of Thomond, and maintained bardic schools that educated generations. In a world obsessed with kingship and conquest, Echtiern's influence was subtle, almost invisible, yet it endured longer than most crowns, including Brian's.

The exact date of Echtiern's death is not known, but because of this very lack of a record, it's likely he died sometime before his more famous brother Brian, who perished in 1014.

The spring of that fateful year was thick with tension. Word had come that the Vikings of Dublin, allied with rebellious Irish lords, were marching toward Clontarf, near the outskirts of Dublin. Brian Boru, now High King of Ireland, knew that the battle ahead would decide the fate of the island for generations.

Echtiern's son, a young man already trained in the ways of memory and poetry must have learned from his (presumably) departed father's legacy of chronicling and took up the pen himself. From the hills overlooking the plain, he could have seen armies arrayed, the glint of axes in the sun, heard the thunder of horses' hooves, the clash of shields and swords.

Brian, fierce and commanding, led his men with the authority of a king who had spent decades uniting a fractured land, though he is estimated to have been near eighty years old by this point. He'd not see his work undone by Norse settlers and their rebellious Gaelic allies.

The battle raged for hours. The air was thick with smoke, dust, and the cries of the wounded. Brian's forces ultimately prevailed, but the tide of war is cruel and impartial. In the chaos of the day, the High King was struck down while praying in his command tent.

As the legend goes, during the Viking retreat, Brodar of Man, a warlord black of heart and thick with rage, stumbled upon Brian's tent on the edge of the field. There, he found Brian, still bent in devotion before the crucifix. With a howl of triumph, Brodar struck. The sword flashed, and the High King fell where he knelt.

Brodar fled, but not far. Brian's men, upon discovering the dark deed, captured him. They tore him to pieces in vengeance, binding his entrails to an oak and driving his body around it in circles until death finally claimed him. Thus did the slayer of Ireland's greatest king perish in a most gruesome torment for his crime. Though differing accounts would later blur the exact details.

With Brian's death, triumph on the battlefield faded into confusion and mourning.

Echtiern's son, perhaps, stood silently among the survivors, quill in hand, heart heavy over the death of his uncle and king. The clash of swords could be forgotten, the cries of dying men silenced by time, but the story must live on. He would have recorded every detail he could: the bravery of warriors, the cunning of Brian's maneuvers, the horror and heroism intertwined on the bloody Clontarf plains.

Through this work, the deeds of his uncle, the great High King of Ireland, were immortalized. The ink traced the memory of a man who had united Ireland, and it traced too, the grief of a family whose patriarch had fallen. Echtiern's sons would ensure that history remembered the triumphs and tragedies, the victories and the sacrifices, of those who shaped Ireland's destiny and to this day, statues stand to commemorate Brian Boru, his likeness stamped on Irish coins. His deeds, legendary.

The quieter labor of the McGraths turned family tragedy into epic, and Clontarf's roar into heroic tales that would persist for a thousand years.

Ultimately, the battle had been a victory for the Dál gCais, quelling Viking power in Ireland forever, but it also left Ireland without a High King and Ireland soon fractured back into regional kingdoms, undoing the dream of a unified Ireland – for the time being.

Through his descendants, Echtiern's influence touched centuries, ensuring that the McGraths would be remembered long after the swords of his brothers fell silent.

The Craith Bard School

In the heart of County Clare, nestled along the banks of the River Fergus, lies the ancient site of Isle McGrath. This serene locale, rich in history, is believed to be the birthplace of the original Craith Bard School, a center of learning and poetic excellence that dates back to the eleventh century and persisted in some form for more than half a millennium. The Mac Craiths were esteemed poets and historians, serving the O'Brien kings of Thomond. Their bardic tradition was not merely a profession but a sacred duty, preserving the annals of their people through verse and song.

The new school was a place where poetry and history intertwined, where sons of the clan learned to memorize genealogies, compose praise poems, and record the deeds of kings and warriors. The early instructors were themselves the family's elders, men who had witnessed Brian Boru's campaigns and could recite Clontarf's saga by heart, passing it to eager pupils.

By the thirteenth century, the Craith Bard School had become the intellectual heart of Thomond.

Seamus Mac Craith, a celebrated poet and teacher of the mid-1200s, was known for his epic verse chronicling the exploits of the O'Brien kings. His students learned not only to write in *dán díreach*, the strict syllabic form of classical Gaelic poetry, but also to mediate disputes between clans by composing genealogical records that determined rights to land and leadership. In these ways, the McGraths wielded cultural power alongside their poetic craft.

In the fifteenth century the school saw figures such as Aenghus Mac Craith (d. 1461), whose satirical poetry could both delight and chastise, holding even nobles to account. His contemporary, Ruaidhri Mac Craith (d. 1491), served as coarb of the Termon of Dabeog, combining ecclesiastical authority with his poetic skill. Ruaidhri's chronicles were widely copied and referenced, cementing the McGraths' reputation not merely as poets but as keepers of law, history, and culture.

By the sixteenth century, the McGraths had established a prominent bardic school in Burgess, South Tipperary. This institution became renowned for its rigorous curriculum, producing scholars who excelled in historical lore and poetry. The school attracted students from across Ireland, eager to learn the art of storytelling and the preservation of history through the poetic form.

The school was by then trying to adapt to a changing Ireland. As Gaelic lords faced pressures from English expansion, the McGraths became hereditary ollamhs, formally recognized as official poets and historians to the O'Briens of Thomond and other noble families. Figures like Muiris Mac Craith, active in the mid-1500s, were instrumental in preserving the oral histories of the Dál gCais at a time when manuscript culture was threatened (and wholesale destruction of Irish records would later ensue). The meticulous chronicles of Muiris included everything from battle accounts to ceremonial genealogies, ensuring that the stories of the clan and its allies would survive both time and conquest.

Ireland's history is marred by tragedies, however and the growing encroachment of English colonial rule and suppression of Gaelic culture in the seventeenth century finally led to the decline of the bardic schools. The Williamite Wars and subsequent policies disrupted the traditional Gaelic way of life, leading to the dispersion of many bardic families and tragically, the loss of a great deal of written lore and oral tradition.

Despite these tragedies, the legacy of the Craith Bard School endures. Today, descendants of the McGrath family continue to honor their ancestors' commitment to the preservation of Irish heritage through poetry and storytelling. The Clan McGrath Society serves as a testament to this enduring legacy, bringing together members from both Thomond and Ulster branches to celebrate and perpetuate the rich bardic traditions of the McGrath clan.

From Thomond, Onward

After the roar of Clontarf faded and the High King Brian Boru fell, Thomond was a land both triumphant and fragile. The Dál gCais had certainly secured their place in history, but the work of preservation of deeds, lineage, and law had only just begun. It was into this world that the Mac Craith clan, descendants of Brian's brother Echtiern, began to stretch their influence.

From Thomond, seat of Dál gCais power, the decedents of Echtiern – the newly named Mac Craith clan eventually spread south to Waterford, where they tended churches and abbeys, and north to Ulster, where they became the guardians of Termonmagrath. Everywhere they went, the echo of Echtiern's quiet legacy followed. No battles were recorded under his name, no epic feats of arms, yet his bloodline became a cornerstone of Irish intellectual and cultural life.

Likely due to the loss of documents over the ages, the earliest surviving written reference to an individual bearing the surname Mac Craith doesn't appear until three hundred years after Brian Boru's death. This early McGrath's first name was sadly not included in the bardic genealogies and annalistic entries of the time. He is referred to only as "Mac Craith, ollamh of the O'Briens." He was thought to be a learned poet and historian who served the Dál gCais kings in the 1300s.

However, despite the lack of recorded individual names, we can track the *clan's* expansion, changing roles and responsibilities.

In Thomond itself, the early Mac Craiths retained their place as hereditary ollamhs – poets, historians, and keepers of genealogies for the O'Briens. But, their talents were needed beyond Clare. Word of their skill in poetry, writing and preserving law spread, and the Mac Craiths were called to other regions, stretching south and east into Waterford and Ulster, becoming stewards of culture wherever Gaelic lords required their knowledge and talents.

When the winds of dynastic strife tore through the Dál gCais in the fourteenth century, a branch of the McGraths loyal to the king of Thomond, Turlough O'Brien, found themselves forced from their ancestral hills. Turlough had been deposed by his brother Mahon, and in the bitter fallout, Turlough and his McGrath supporters crossed the mountains into Waterford, settling near the harbor town of Dungarvan, where the marshy riverbank promised refuge, commerce, and safety.

There, on the ancient footprint of an old Gaelic fort, the McGraths raised their stronghold: McGrath Castle, and beside it, an Augustinian abbey that became their spiritual center. The O'Briens and McGraths would be both the protectors and the patrons of the abbey, binding their fate together with faith.

Waterford offered fertile lands and towns eager for learned advisers and skilled scribes. The McGraths arrived not as wanton conquerors, but reluctantly, as keepers of history, law, and spirituality, a subtle power that would endure there for generations.

Today, little remains of McGrath Castle in Dungarvan – a few stones, old drawings, and the echo of its once-proud presence. But the spirit of that McGrath-O'Brien alliance endures through the Abbeyside district's name, and where McGrath bones lie beneath the earth.

One of the most notable figures to arise in this new southern branch was Philip McGrath, who in 1628 had Sleady Castle constructed, near Lismore. Sleady was more than a home; it was a symbol of the family's permanence and prestige in the region. From its towers, the McGraths maintained the threads of Gaelic culture, even as the tides of Norman influence and English governance sought to reshape the south of Ireland.

According to local legend, Sleady Castle was built to satisfy the high standards of Philip's bride, who had little interest in moving into a simple farmhouse. She demanded walls of stone, high chimneys, and gables that spoke of permanence and prestige. And so began the long labor of Sleady Castle, which rose from the earth stone by stone until its tall silhouette commanded the countryside near Cappoquin.

When the castle was completed, it was more than a residence. It was a declaration that the McGraths, poets and historians by heritage, could also be builders of stone. Not only keepers of words, they would also be keepers of keeps! Oddly enough, after all the expense, Philip's wealth was said to grow considerably as construction went on, as if the land itself had rewarded his faith in Sleady's walls.

But Ireland's peace was fragile. Only a generation later, fortune turned. The rising tide of English power in Munster brought with it the iron hand of confiscation. Like so many Gaelic strongholds, Sleady Castle fell victim not to siege or cannon, but to law and decree. Under the expanding system of Plantation, Catholic families of long inheritance found their rights stripped away and their lands granted to English settlers loyal to the Crown. The McGraths, though rooted in Waterford for centuries, were no exception.

Sleady was seized and passed into the hands of strangers, its walls still fresh with the pride of Philip's vision. For the

McGraths, the loss was more than stone and soil. It was a wound to identity and pride.

The McGraths were driven from Sleady, their goods plundered, their legacy at the mercy of a foreign power. The English Crown granted the castle to Sir Richard Osborne, and the proud McGrath residence became another spoil of conquest.

A castle that had stood as proof of their permanence became a symbol of dispossession, an injustice that echoed through the years to immediately follow and helped stoke the fires of rebellion that soon swept across the British Isles leading to the "Eleven Year" Confederate Wars that would begin with the Irish Rebellion of 1641.

For centuries after, Sleady lingered as a shadow of its former self – gables cracked, chimneys hollow, the music of its halls replaced by the cry of crows, but Sleady Castle still stands as a mostly-in-tact ruin and the current owners, the Hickey family graciously open it up to Clan McGrath events.

Despite ever-increasing English oppression, before and after Philip's time, Waterford McGraths served as hereditary ollamhs, the learned poets and chroniclers of noble families. They recorded the genealogies of local lords, chronicled battles, and composed elegies and praise poetry that celebrated valor, loyalty, and lineage. These works were carefully preserved, ensuring that the deeds of both the O'Briens and the McGraths themselves would be remembered.

The family also left its mark in the church. Several McGraths entered the clergy, overseeing abbeys and parish lands, managing records of land ownership, and adjudicating disputes. Their authority was rooted in knowledge: a McGrath's word carried weight because it came backed by generations of scholarship and precise record-keeping.

The McGraths of Waterford combined intellect, tradition, and quiet influence. From Thomond's hills to Sleady Castle, their legacy endured in the written word, the guidance of lords, and the preservation of Gaelic culture.

To the east, in Ulster, expanding branches of the family took up similar roles. They were keepers of law and tradition, mediating disputes and ensuring that records of inheritance, land claims, and noble deeds were accurate. Yet in Ulster, the McGraths would become far more than wandering poets; they would carve out a role of both spiritual and political weight that endured for centuries. Wherever they went, the Mac Craiths carried with them a simple but profound ethos: memory was power, and the pen could preserve what the sword could not.

By the late medieval period, the McGraths had established themselves around Lough Derg in County Donegal, where they became the hereditary guardians of Saint Patrick's Purgatory. This famed pilgrimage site drew lords, peasants, and even kings from across Europe, all seeking penance and visions in its rocky chambers. And at the heart of it stood the McGraths, custodians of the holy place, trusted with its administration and its legends. In a world where the line between faith and politics blurred, this was no small power. The McGraths controlled who came, who paid, and whose prayers were heard.

Beyond their ecclesiastical role, the Ulster McGraths were entwined with the great families of the north, especially the O'Neills. They served as advisers and keepers of genealogies, ensuring the O'Neill lords could trace their claim to kingship back through the mists of time. In councils and courts, a McGrath's recitation of lineage could steady the legitimacy of a ruler... or unsettle it.

The family also raised castles of their own in the region. Ruins attributed to the Clan McGrath still dot Fermanagh and Donegal, reminders that even poets and priests could hold stone strongholds when needed. These fortresses were less symbols of conquest than of guardianship. These outposts of the McGrath legacy, watched over holy ground and family lands alike.

When a priest named Miler McGrath (much more will be told about this infamous character in the following chapters) rose from the quiet guardianship of Lough Derg to become one of the most powerful bishops in Ireland, he knew that words and titles alone were not enough. To secure his family's place in history, he needed a fortress to anchor the McGrath name in the landscape of Ulster. And so, in the late sixteenth century, he ordered the building of Castle McGrath in County Donegal, near Pettigo, not far from the sacred waters of Lough Derg (some accounts attribute the construction to Miler's son, James).

The castle was originally a stout, four-story tower house, its thick walls rising above the surrounding woods and fields. It was more than a residence; it was a declaration that the McGraths were no longer merely custodians of holy sites or poets in the service of kings. They were landholders, lords in their own right. For generations after Miler, Castle McGrath stood as the seat of the family's northern branch, guarding both their estates and their influence over the pilgrims who continued to flock to nearby Saint Patrick's Purgatory.

But Ireland's peace was never steady. The Williamite Wars of the late seventeenth century brought ruin to countless Gaelic families, and Castle McGrath was not spared. During the turmoil, it was attacked and burned by militia loyal to England, its proud walls blackened by fire, its inhabitants scattered. Like Sleady Castle in Waterford, it fell victim to the great political storms that swept across the island, leaving behind only a ruin to tell of former grandeur.

Today, only about half of Castle McGrath remains standing in a remote sheep pasture. Its weathered beige stones stained and overgrown with weeds and grass, a lonely monument to Miler's ambition and the clan's turbulent fortunes during the 1600s. There have been numerous unrealized plans to restore the castle, but like Sleady Castle, Castle McGrath's current landlords occasionally open the property for Clan McGrath gatherings.

By the sixteenth and seventeenth centuries, as Ulster was convulsed by political oppression and rebellion, the McGraths of the north remained remarkably steadfast. Some aligned with the Gaelic lords in resistance, while others, like their Waterford kin, adapted to survive under English encroachment. Yet through all upheaval, they remained tied to Lough Derg, their role as keepers of the pilgrimage enduring well into the modern era.

Thus, the story of the McGraths in Ulster is not one of fleeting presence, but of anchoring roots. In the south, their name was sung in poetry and stone castles; in the north, it was whispered in prayers and carved into holy ledgers. Together, these branches kept the clan alive.

A Passage to the Afterlife: Saint Patrick's Purgatory

In the mist-shrouded wilds of County Donegal, on the lonely waters of Lough Derg, there lies a small, wind-bitten island that has drawn pilgrims, poets, and penitent kings for more than a thousand years. Known as St. Patrick's Purgatory, this stark outcrop – barely a few acres of rock and bog – became one of the most extraordinary sacred sites in all of Christendom. Here, legend claims, St. Patrick himself descended into the mouth of Purgatory to witness the torments of the damned and the glory of the redeemed, in visions so powerful it was said to convert even the hardest hearts of pagan Ireland.

The story begins in the fifth century, when Patrick, weary from his mission to bring the faith to Ireland's northern tribes, prayed for a sign that would strengthen his followers' belief. God, it was said, revealed to him a cave on an island in Lough Derg – a crevice in the island's bedrock that would lead Patrick to the spirit realm. Patrick entered it, spent a night in its depths, and emerged transformed. The place became known as *Teampall Phádraig:* St. Patrick's Chapel and word of the holy site would later spread across medieval Europe like fire on heather, but not until about a half-millennium after Patrick's life and times.

The medieval Irish would not have called it "Purgatory," at the time. They had no need of such a word. The Catholic notion of a spiritual holding cell called "Purgatory" didn't emerge until the thirteenth century. In the oldest Latin, *purgatorium* meant simply a place of purification. And that is what this cavern *may* have originally been – a sweathouse, or something very much like it used to purge and heal. A *teach allais,* a low or subterranean stone chamber, in common use into the twentieth century, was old Ireland's medicine room. The fires inside released the curative spirits of herbs; the heat drove out sickness, sorrow, and whatever unnamed darkness lay within. Within the cramped hollows, they would sit or lie amid the rising smoke, sweating and coughing, waiting for their aches to leave them. It was a place not of punishment, but of purging – a cleansing of the body and, perhaps, the soul.

It likely wasn't until the twelfth century that St. Patrick's Purgatory become world-renowned as a place of pilgrimage rivaling Rome and Jerusalem, as the tale of Saint Patrick's spiritual visions reached Europe.

The McGrath clan held sway over the land at that time, and the McGraths have long been remembered as poets, bards and storytellers. No doubt, these crafty wordsmiths played a role in popularizing and disseminating the legend of St. Patrick's Purgatory. It's earliest mention in surviving texts occurs in 1185 (though it is important to remember that wholesale destruction of Irish records and manuscripts swept across the Emerald Isle in the seventeenth century).

Many knights and noblemen traveled from France, Spain, and even Hungary to endure the brutal vigil of purification, days of fasting, prayer, and sleepless penitence, locked in the darkness of the cave. Chroniclers described pilgrims trembling in awe as the monks sealed a heavy stone door, leaving them to face the visions of their own sins. It has been suggested that Dante himself could have drawn inspiration for his *Inferno* from tales of the Donegal underworld.

The McGraths of Termonmagrath, hereditary keepers of the island, held guardianship over this sacred site for centuries. It was they who protected the pilgrims, managed the lands of the termon (church territory), collected offerings and kept order among the penitents. Their charge was both an honor and a spiritual burden – one that tied the McGraths not just to the land, but to the very border between life and death, heaven and hell.

Their ancestral lands formed a protective ring around the holy island, and the title – Coarb of St. Patrick's Purgatory – marked them as the guardians of one of Ireland's most venerated pilgrimage sites.

Historical records trace this stewardship to at least the Twelfth Century, when the McGraths were recognized as the *erenaghs* (church landholders) responsible for maintaining a monastery built on the island and welcoming pilgrims. The Annals of the Four Masters and other monastic accounts refer to Termonmagrath – literally "the sanctuary of the McGraths" – as both a spiritual refuge and a stronghold of Gaelic tradition. But their charge was not without peril. The McGraths' position as guardians of the termon lands made them targets during periods of English expansion. Even as they fought to preserve the faith, they also defended the autonomy of their people.

The site endured storms of both weather and politics. In 1632, an English protestant governor, viewing the pilgrimage as a source of troublesome "Catholic superstition," ordered the cave destroyed and the friars expelled. The cavern itself was filled in, but still the pilgrims returned, undeterred, praying around the mound that once held the cave – now marked by a tall tower. Over time, new chapels rose, the tradition continued, and the legend refused to die. Today, Station Island – as it is now called – hums with devotion every summer, when pilgrims walk the same rough stones trodden by their ancestors, circling the *penitential beds* in silence, whispering prayers into the Donegal wind.

For over fifteen centuries, St. Patrick's Purgatory has remained a threshold between worlds, a place where even the hardest hearts might glimpse eternity – or at least seek forgiveness for their sins. With the closure of the cavern, the focus of the island changed from seeking visions of the other realm to quiet contemplation and atonement.

Right by Station Island lies Saint's Island, another important historical and religious site associated with St. Patrick's Purgatory. Saint's Island was the home of the original monastery that looked after the Purgatory. There, many McGrath caretakers, Augustinian monks and Terminors, are buried.

Today, nearly the whole of the small Station Island is occupied by impressive stone structures – a monastery, a basilica, a dormitory for pilgrims and broad docks to accommodate visitors arriving by boat.

Miler McGrath: A Catholic and a Protestant

In the year 1523, in the shadow of the Blue Stack Mountains of Donegal, Miler McGrath was born into a family whose name carried weight in both faith and scholarship. The McGraths of Ulster were the hereditary custodians of Saint Patrick's Purgatory at Lough Derg, guardians of a holy site that drew pilgrims from across Europe. From an early age, Miler would have seen travelers kneeling on the rocky island, fasting, praying, and begging for salvation. He would have well understood that his family's role straddled the line between the sacred and the worldly.

Miler pursued the holy life in earnest. He joined the Franciscan order, dedicating himself to study and to the rhythm of monastic devotion. In 1565, he was appointed Catholic Bishop of Down and Connor, a very high and honorable station in the Church and with great influence in Earthly affairs. And Miler was no ordinary churchman. His eyes were set not only on heaven, but on the shifting powers of Ireland itself.

The sixteenth century was an age of upheaval. The Reformation had splintered Christendom, and the English Crown sought to tighten its grip on Ireland, replacing Gaelic lords and Catholic bishops with loyal Protestant rulers. Into this storm stepped Miler, who did what few of his contemporaries dared: he switched sides. By 1567, he had conformed to the new (Anglican) Church of Ireland and was rewarded with the bishopric of Clogher.

From there, his rise was astonishing. He accumulated ecclesiastical titles like a chieftain gathered cattle. By 1571, he was Archbishop of Cashel, one of the greatest sees in Ireland. At the height of his career, he held no fewer than four bishoprics at once, a feat unheard of. His revenues were vast, his power unmatched among clerics.

But his compromises made him enemies on all sides. To Catholic Ireland, he was a traitor: a man who had abandoned the Holy Roman Church for the lure of English gold. To Protestants, he was suspect. He was a Gaelic-born Catholic prelate whose loyalty was never entirely trusted. Among his own Franciscan brothers, he was condemned as a renegade. Yet Miler endured. He navigated rebellion, English plantation, and the long shadow of Elizabethan rule, always keeping his seat, always guarding his fortunes.

For a time, Miler actually held titles from both churches simultaneously. His dual and competing bishoprics were nothing short of scandalous in sixteenth-century Ireland. At a time when the island was torn between loyalty to Rome and submission to the English Crown, Miler attempted to sit astride both worlds. As Catholic Bishop of Down and Connor, he was expected to defend the authority of the Pope; yet he had also accepted the Protestant bishopric of Clogher from Queen Elizabeth. For a period, he collected revenues from both churches at once, a brazen act that outraged Catholics, who saw betrayal, and unsettled Protestants, who doubted his sincerity. The spectacle of one man claiming allegiance to two conflicting faiths, and profiting handsomely from both, made Miler infamous, a figure whispered about in taverns and cursed in pulpits, embodying both the corruption and the survivalism of his age.

In the closing years of the sixteenth century, when his fortunes were at their height, Miler McGrath ordered the raising of a stronghold near Pettigo in County Donegal. It would be known as Castle McGrath. Rising four stories above the countryside, the tower house was both fortress and family seat, its thick stone walls a declaration that the McGraths, once guardians of pilgrims at Lough Derg, were now lords in their own right. From its windows, Miler's kin looked out over their lands and the holy lake beyond, a reminder that their influence reached across both the spiritual and physical worlds. Miler himself went on to take up residence in the much grander Lismore Castle while Archbishop of Cashel.

But the safety and fortune that Miler carved out for his family was not untouchable. A century later, Ireland was in flames and Castle McGrath, once a symbol of permanence, was caught in the storm. Attacked and burned by a Protestant militia, its walls blackened and its halls left hollow, the once proud stronghold fell into ruin (Lismore Castle still stands in exemplary condition to this day, however).

Miler McGrath's legacy is a paradox. To some, he remains a symbol of betrayal, a bishop who sold his soul for land and title. To others, he was a pragmatist, a survivor who preserved his family's fortune through Ireland's most dangerous century. Either way, he is remembered as the most controversial of all McGraths, whose name still echoes whenever the clan's history is told.

Miler lived to the extraordinary age of 100 years, dying in 1622, a survivor in a century that consumed most men long before their time. When asked near the end of his life how he managed to hold his place through wars, rebellions, and the fury of both churches, he reportedly replied, "It is the will of God that I should live; and I live still."

High on the limestone outcrop of the Rock of Cashel, where round towers, ruined chapels, elaborate grave markers and the broken ribs of soaring Gothic arches rise against the sky, lies the final resting place of Miler McGrath. The Rock was once the seat of the kings of Munster, later claimed by the church as one of Ireland's most sacred sites. For centuries it had been the stage of coronations, conversions, and battles of faith. To be buried here was no ordinary honor. It was a statement of power, legacy, and of belonging to the great story of Ireland.

Miler's grave lies among bishops and archbishops, men who had guided the church through wars and reformations. His presence there is both fitting and ironic: fitting, because as Archbishop of Cashel he held sway over the great fortress-turned-cathedral for decades; ironic, because his life was one of controversy, straddling Catholic and Protestant loyalties, loved by few but feared by many. Yet in death, he claimed a place at Ireland's spiritual heart, where his name would not be forgotten. The Rock of Cashel, towering over the Golden Vale, ensures that Miler McGrath's memory remains bound not only to scandal, but to stone and legend, resting amid the ruins and remains of kings and saints.

Plantation

When the English Crown spoke of "plantation," they did not mean gardens or crops but the planting of people. Settlers loyal to the Crown were relocated to establish roots in confiscated Irish soil. The concept was vile, ruthless, and also tragically effective: displace the native Gaelic families who had ruled their lands for centuries, seize their castles and fields, and resettle them with English and Scottish Protestants. It was both a military strategy and a cultural experiment, meant to tame a land that had resisted English control for generations.

Recall the 1995 film Braveheart, when King Edward The Longshanks declared, "The trouble with Scotland, is that it's full of Scots." It was this exact line of thinking behind King James' Plantation of Ulster: "De-Irish" Ireland by replacing prominent Irish families with English loyalists.

By the early 1600s, after the defeat of great Gaelic lords like Hugh O'Neill and Red Hugh O'Donnell, the policy of plantation was carried out with merciless efficiency in Ulster, Ireland's most northern province (six of Ulster's nine counties now comprise Northern Ireland, which to this day remains part of the United Kingdom, even after the rest of the island finally gained independence).

For the McGraths of Donegal and Fermanagh, plantation was a catastrophe. The clan had long held the title of hereditary

Termoners of Lough Derg, guardians of the holy pilgrimage site known as Saint Patrick's Purgatory. That role gave them spiritual influence and practical power, since pilgrims from across Ireland and beyond passed through McGrath lands and paid their dues. Allied with the O'Donnells, the McGraths had built Castle McGrath near the lake in the late sixteenth century, a sturdy stone keep that symbolized their strength and their place in the Gaelic order. For a time, their power seemed unshakable.

When the Plantation of Ulster began in 1609, the Crown held next to no regard for Gaelic titles or centuries of custom. Lands were confiscated wholesale, and settlers arrived with papers bearing royal seals aimed at uprooting Gaelic tradition and culture.

Though Archbishop Miler McGrath, ever the pragmatist, managed to secure pardons for parts of his extended family in 1608, that protection would not endure forever. English garrisons and Scottish planters arrived, carving up the countryside that had once bowed to Gaelic chiefs. The McGraths, like so many others, found their privileges eroded, their ancestral rights challenged, their stronghold increasingly isolated.

The final blow came during the chaos of the mid-seventeenth century. The Irish Confederate Wars erupted in 1641, part rebellion, part civil war, and part proxy battle between the English king and Parliament. In this maelstrom, the McGraths sided with the rebellion against the Crown and Castle McGrath stood as both fortress and target. Turlough McGrath, Miler's grandson was Chieftain at the time and he led 140 rebels in the conflict, which brought the battle home to Termonmagrath. The Lagganers, a pro-Crown militia drawn from Protestant settler families, attacked with fire and steel. McGrath castle was besieged and burned, its stones left blackened against the Donegal sky. With its fall, the clan's dwindling hold on Ulster was finally broken.

What plantation had begun, dispossessing and displacing the old Gaelic order in Ulster, the destruction of Castle McGrath punctuated.

Scattered by fire and conquest, the McGraths of Ulster faced a choice common to many Gaelic families in the wake of plantation: to bend, to fight, or to flee. Some remained near Lough Derg, clinging to their hereditary role as guides of the pilgrimage. Even as English officials claimed ownership of the land, pilgrims still whispered that it was the McGraths who knew the sacred island best, who kept alive the prayers and customs that had outlasted kings.

Others turned to the pen and the pulpit. In keeping with their bardic tradition, some McGraths continued on in the region as poets, chroniclers, and priests, keeping alive the Gaelic tongue in defiance of English suppression. Manuscripts from the seventeenth and eighteenth centuries mention McGraths as scribes, carrying the memory of Brian Boru's lineage and the old heroic tales forward into new generations.

Famine would later accelerate migration out of Ireland, but many displaced McGrath's began to emigrate in the wake of the Plantation of Ulster.

The once-proud custodians of Lough Derg were scattered, their influence reduced to memory and manuscript. Yet the family name, the stories, the poems and songs endured. The evolving history of the clan continued on in parish records, rebel musters, and emigrant ships. Plantation had stripped the Ulster McGraths of land, but not of lineage.

Those who remained didn't pass up opportunity to take up arms again when the occasions arose. McGraths appear in rebel lists during the 1641 Rising, and again during the Williamite Wars at the end of the seventeenth century. The McGrath chieftain, Brian (son of Turlough and great grandson of Miler) stood alongside the Jacobites who sought to restore Catholic sovereignty in Ireland and was branded an outlaw when that rebellion was crushed. Though often on the losing side, the McGraths stood up again and again. Rebellion became part of the family story.

The effect of Plantation stretched beyond Ulster, of course. In the southeast, the times carried the same iron weight: confiscation, colonization, and control. The McGraths of Waterford, lords of their own stone keeps, found themselves in their own struggle against the tightening grip of the English Crown.

By the sixteenth century, the McGraths of Waterford had risen as a powerful branch of the clan. They were tied to the great Geraldine earls of Desmond, acting as allies, fosters, and protectors in Munster's tangled world of Gaelic and Anglo-Norman rivalry. Around Sleady Castle, the McGraths watched over rich valleys and commanded the respect of their neighbors. But when the Desmond Rebellions (1569–1583) broke out, the McGraths were swept into the storm. The English Crown, determined to crush Catholic resistance in Munster, declared war not just on the Geraldines but on their allies as well.

The aftermath was catastrophic. With the defeat of the Desmond earls, vast tracts of Munster were seized and earmarked for the Plantation of Munster. English adventurers and loyal Protestant settlers were granted confiscated lands, while families like the McGraths were branded rebels, their titles stripped, their castles marked for destruction.

Sleady Castle, once a proud seat, was battered in these wars, and the McGrath presence in Waterford was diminished, yet not all was lost. Unlike in Ulster, where settlers poured in and Gaelic families were forced from their heartlands almost overnight, in Waterford the mountains and valleys provided a degree of cover.

Some McGrath families adapted by entering into uneasy agreements with Crown officials, or converting land ownership into leases under English law. Others simply endured in the hills and mountains, stubbornly holding on to what scraps they could. In this way, the Waterford McGraths survived plantation not by open defiance, but by resilience, compromise, and a keen instinct for survival.

By the seventeenth century, the Waterford McGraths had lost much of their old independence, but their name endured in the hills and parishes. They lived on as tenants, priests, poets, and, when the chance came, rebels. Plantation may have humbled, but not erased them and they lived on to fight back when the time was ripe.

Meanwhile, even the McGrath's Dalcassian ancestral home high in the rolling hills of Thomond was not spared the Crown's unholy attention.

The Plantation of Munster and the wider English colonial agenda swept through the south and west, targeting Gaelic lords and their allies. The Thomond McGraths, who had prospered in the old order, found themselves caught between Crown mandates and loyalty to their patrons. English officials claimed that the lands of Thomond were ripe for "settlement," and grant letters soon appeared in Dublin, naming English and Scottish settlers as the new rightful owners of property long held by McGraths.

The Thomond McGraths, hereditary bards and scribes were masters of laws and deeds and some McGraths used their skills to seek accommodation. With diplomacy and pragmatism, they negotiated leases or accepted nominal titles under English law, preserving some fragments of their estates.

They also took up their bardic pens, composing poems of lament for lost castles, ruined churches, and dispossessed kin. These poems were more than art. They were weapons of memory, encoding the clan's defiance and identity at a time when Gaelic swords and castles had been largely stripped away.

The McGraths' bardic school survived for a time as a focal point of cultural resistance. There, poetry and music preserved the history of the Dál gCais, Brian Boru, historical alliances, and the injustices wrought by plantation. Manuscripts from the era, often copied in secret, recorded praises for fallen Gaelic lords, elegies for destroyed castles, and laments over the spiritual cost of conquest. Much of that work still survives in museums, the National Library of Ireland and the grand and expansive library at Trinity College in Dublin.

The Thomond McGraths survived the initial waves of plantation, though by the end of the seventeenth century, much of their political power had vanished. They remained priests, poets, and educators, ensuring that Counties Clare and Limerick would not forget the Gaelic order that once governed the green hills and winding rivers in the west of Ireland. Plantation had tried, but it could not erase the McGrath legacy, which endured through song, story, the bardic tradition and the sacred waters of Lough Derg.

Ill-Fated Rebellion

The wind tore across the green hills of Ulster and Munster, carrying the restless whispers of a people long bruised by English conquest and oppression. For centuries, the McGraths held positions of respect and authority in the north and south of Ireland. Custodians of Lough Derg in Thomond, lords of valleys near Waterford, keepers of castles and holy sites. But the Plantation, wars, and confiscations had scattered them, leaving only traces of their once proud authority. By 1798, the memory of lost ancestral lands and broken castles still burned bright in the hearts of those who carried the McGrath name.

Across the island, a new fire was kindling. Inspired by newly won American Independence and revolutionary fervor in France, whispers of liberty and equality swept through the United Irishmen. Among them was Patrick McGrath, a man of fierce courage and deep ties to the old Gaelic order. Born into the Waterford McGraths, he remembered tales of Sleady Castle, of hilltop pastures stolen during the Munster Plantation, of priests and poets who had preserved the clan's honor in exile and manuscript. His mission was clear: rise, strike, and reclaim some measure of justice for the generations who had lost so much.

Rebellion erupted in May 1798. From Waterford's rolling hills to the plains of Ulster, McGraths took up arms with allied clans as United Irishmen. Patrick led a band of insurgents through familiar terrain once walked by his forebearers, striking at English garrisons and loyalist strongholds. Fires raged in the towns, musket smoke mingled with the scent of spring grass, and the old stories of castle sieges and bardic lamentations came alive again in every skirmish.

Yet, despite courage and cunning, the rebellion faltered. The Crown's troops were ruthless, and rebel coordination proved insufficient against the superior power of a professional military and artillery. Many McGraths fought valiantly, some fell on the field, others were captured, their names etched in local memory as martyrs for freedom. Patrick McGrath himself became a symbol, remembered not just for his deeds in battle, but for embodying centuries of McGrath resilience, the undying loyalty to clan and country, and the indomitable spirit of those whose lands had once stretched from Thomond to Waterford.

When the smoke cleared, the rebellion had failed, but the spirit of resistance endured. In every valley, hill, ruined castle and churchyard, the determination for Irish independence remained. Indeed, the Irish fought the English for centuries and were never completely bowed. Five years later, that spark of rebellion flared up again.

The streets of Dublin were dark and tense on the night of July 23rd, 1803. Lanterns swung in the wind, casting flickering shadows on the cobblestones. The city's elite slept, unaware that rebellion was stirring in their midst. Robert Emmet, barely twenty-five but already famed for his eloquence and daring, moved through the darkened lanes with the precision of a general and the fire of a revolutionary. He had inherited the dream of the United Irishmen, carrying forward the hopes of those who had risen – and fallen – back in 1798.

Emmet's plan was audacious. Small bands of men were to seize key government offices, spark an uprising, and rally the people of

Dublin in a single, decisive strike. The streets would become a battlefield, the air alive with the shouts of insurgents and the clash of steel.

But fate, and betrayal, were swift. A gun misfired in one alley, confusion spread among the insurgents, and panic replaced courage. The rebellion faltered almost before it began. Troops loyal to the Crown surged through the streets, cutting down rebels with cold efficiency. Emmet, realizing the effort had failed, slipped away into the night, the weight of a nation's hope pressing on his shoulders.

He was betrayed, captured, and imprisoned. In the Tower of Dublin, he wrote letters that would echo through history, explaining that his rebellion was not born of recklessness but of necessity.

Tried and found guilty of treason, the court was silent as Emmet, pale but resolute, addressed the judge and jury. As he was about to be condemned to death, his voice remained steady yet burning with indignation.

"Let no man write my epitaph. The cause I die for is the cause of Ireland. Let it be said that Robert Emmet, though failing in the attempt to rouse his countrymen, fell faithful to her liberty. My friends, my fellow-countrymen, do not despair. The day will come when Ireland shall be free. I leave my body to the grave, but my spirit, my hopes, and my heart remain with the people," he said.

Emmet spoke not only as a rebel but as a visionary, framing his death as a symbol of resistance rather than defeat. His words resonated far beyond the walls of the court and his spirit of rebellion lived on in the face of continued oppression.

On September 20th, 1803, Robert Emmet was executed, standing tall before the gallows, refusing to kneel, his stirring words a testament to the bent but unbroken cause of Irish freedom.

Though the rebellion itself was crushed in a single night, Emmet became a legend. His courage inspired poets and balladeers with McGraths naturally among the chroniclers that gave hope and vision to generations of Irish patriots. Rebellion had been crushed by the English to this point, but it was far from over.

Mrs. McGrath

At the dawn of the Nineteenth Century, Europe trembled under the hoofbeats of Napoleon Bonaparte's Grande Armée. One by one, kingdoms toppled or bent the knee. British ministers warned that if France crossed the English Channel, England itself could fall – and Ireland, Britain's uneasy and rather unwilling partner, could be the first battlefield.

To the Irish, Napoleon was not just a tyrant across the sea. He was also something of a distant hope. France had supported Irish rebels in 1798, and many believed Napoleon might free Ireland from British rule if he invaded. London knew this well. Fear of French incursion turned every Irish harbor into a military priority and every Irishman into a potential threat… or an expendable soldier.

And so the great recruiting machine rolled into motion. The English came with beating drums, crisp uniforms with bright buttons and promises: regular pay, hot meals, adventure, and a chance to prove Irish bravery on the grand European stage. But for many recruits, the real reason to enlist was simpler: the King's shilling meant survival. A hungry man with no prospects saw the army as the only employer willing to take him.

By 1810, nearly one in five soldiers in the British Army was Irish – a staggering proportion considering Ireland's population and its political grievances. Regiments like the Connaught Rangers and the Royal Irish Fusiliers became feared shock troops, celebrated for their ferocity in battle and cursed for their expendability.

The war that awaited them was a hellscape stretching across Portugal and Spain. The British Army's supreme strategist, the future Duke of Wellington, relied heavily on Irish regiments to form his backbone.

When the war finally ended in 1815 with Napoleon's defeat at Waterloo, thousands of Irish veterans returned home. Some came back proud; many came back broken. Cripples missing limbs, men haunted by the horrors of siege warfare, soldiers who had marched across half of Europe only to confront once more the poverty they had joined the army to escape and continue to live as less than free men under the English boot suppressing Ireland.

The popular Irish folk song, Mrs. McGrath memorialized the sentiment of the time.

Now Mrs. McGrath, the sergeant said;
Would you like to make a soldier out of your son Ted?
With scarlet coat and cockade hat;
Now Mrs. McGrath wouldn't you like that?

[Chorus]
With your too-ri-a, fol-di-diddle-da, too-ri, oor-ri, oor-ri-a;
With your too-ri-a, fol-di-diddle-da, too-ri, oor-ri, oor-ri-a

So, Mrs. McGrath stayed by the shore;
Waiting for her son for seven years or more;
Till she saw a ship sailing into the bay;
Here's my son Ted now *má's eadh* clear the way

Captain dear where have you been;

Have you been sailing on the Med-it-tare-a-e-in?
Have you got news of my son Ted?
Is the poor fellow living or is he dead?

Then up came Ted without any legs;
Walking on a pair of wooden pegs;
She kissed him a dozen times or two;
Mother of God, sure it can't be you

Were you drunk or were you blind;
When you left your two fine legs behind;
Or was it walking on the say;
Took your two fine legs from the knees away

No I wasn't drunk and I wasn't blind;
When I left my two fine legs behind;
But a cannonball on the fifth of May;
Took my fine legs from the knees away

Oh Teddy McGrath the widow cried;
Your fine legs were your mothers' pride;
Them stumps of trees won't do at all;
Why didn't you run from the cannonball?

All foreign wars I do proclaim;
Between Don Juan and the King of Spain;
I'd rather have my Teddy as he used to be;
Than the King of France and his whole navy

The song, by an unknown writer was later known to be the
most popular marching song among the Irish volunteers of World
War I.

Famine

The Great Irish Famine (1845–1852) was one of the most devastating tragedies in modern Europe. Known in Irish as *An Gorta Mór* ("the Great Hunger"), it began when a blight struck the potato, the staple crop of Ireland's poor. Entire fields blackened and rotted in the ground, leaving millions without their primary source of food. A million died, and over a million more fled across the Atlantic in a desperate exodus. But while the blight was a natural disaster, the famine itself was not inevitable. It was exacerbated, prolonged, worsened and some would say *caused* by English policies that certainly turned hardship into catastrophe.

For centuries before the famine, Ireland had been reshaped by Plantation and English land confiscation. Vast tracts of fertile farmland had been seized from Irish families and given to English landlords. Irish tenants were forced onto smaller, poorer plots, where the potato, nutritious, hardy, and high-yield, became their only lifeline. When the potato blight came, it struck precisely where it could do the most damage: among those who had nothing else to eat.

The cruel irony was that Ireland was still producing an abundance of quality food – just not for the Irish. Across the countryside, Irish farmers labored on fertile estates, raising grain, beef, pork, sheep and dairy of the highest quality, but these goods were sent eastward, and loaded onto ships bound for English markets. Military escorts often protected the shipments, ensuring that export quotas were met even as the Irish poor literally starved at the very gates of the storehouses. Thus, the soil of Ireland yielded plenty, but the people who tilled it were left with nothing but the blackened husks of their devastated potato crops.

The British government's response was a mixture of neglect and unwavering ideology. Influenced by laissez-faire economics, officials insisted the market would correct itself, refusing to interfere in food distribution. Relief efforts, when they came, were scant and riddled with cruelty: workhouses where families were split apart, soup kitchens that offered watery broth in exchange for conversion to the English brand of Protestantism, and public works schemes that demanded backbreaking labor from starving men for a few pennies' pay. The policies betrayed a chilling and heartless logic: better to let hunger break the Irish than to question the sanctity of English landlords and empire.

As starvation worsened, Ireland emptied. Despairing and with no good options remaining, over a million souls boarded coffin ships. These were overcrowded, poorly provisioned vessels that carried starving emigrants to America, Canada, and Australia, with many dying before even reaching the far shores.

Villages vanished, fields went untended, and once-vibrant communities fell silent. The famine was not merely a tragedy of nature. It was the culmination of centuries of dispossession, enforced by English governance that valued export profits and political control of the fertile Emerald Isle over Irish lives.

The mass exodus, coupled with over a million starvation deaths, cut Ireland's population by nearly a quarter in less than a decade. It was a demographic collapse from which the island never fully recovered. The Great Irish Famine reshaped Ireland forever. It fueled bitterness against England, hardened nationalist resolve, and scattered the Irish across the globe. Yet in the songs, poems, and stories that survived, the memory of the famine became not only a record of suffering but a warning: of what happens when a people are denied sovereignty over their own destiny. Later, they would also become a rallying cry.

During this tragic period of Irish history between Plantation and famine, the once learned and influential McGraths were reduced to poverty. Perhaps not all, but many. Records of relief and emigration assistance during this time paint a bleak picture for the McGraths.

At dawn, Bridget McGrath of Cappagh awoke to find her potato beds still black with blight, her children crying with empty bellies and threadbare clothes. She had once dreamed of sending one of her sons across the water where food was said to be abundant. According to the records, one August in the 1850s, with nothing left, Bridget accepted the meager relief offer of £4 (and/or clothes) from the Dungarvan Guardians.

In another record, we find Margaret McGrath, mother of four, given £26.12 to fund her family's emigration to America. She left behind smoky chimneys, torn fences, and a field she could not farm, but took hope in the promise of a better life for her family in the United States – if they would survive the journey.

In County Clare, near the hills of Kilshanny, a group of McGrath siblings (young and old) folded their lives into trunks and boarded a ship bound for Axedale in Victoria, Australia. The famine years had left their land in tatters; the rent demand hid in every shadow. Australia was far, terrifyingly far, but also full of sunlight, promise, and the chance to live without hunger.

When Mary Anne McGrath, just eighteen years old, sailed from Queenstown for Chicago, Illinois, she carried not only her few belongings, but the weight of generations crushed under failing crops, eviction notices, and starving neighbors. In her letters home, she would speak of poverty and sorrow, but also of survival. She would plant a new life among American strangers.

These McGraths were not renowned in the annals of history – no glorious battles, no famous elegies or scrolls of royal lineage. They represent many ordinary McGraths whose lives were torn apart. Yet together, their departures numbered in the thousands; each emigration certificate, each passage ticket, each name in a relief ledger represents a small tragedy and for some, a great hope.

The famine years were a breaking point, in more ways than one. The potato blight returned season after season, leaving only rotting crops in the ground, Many McGraths left Ireland, but still, many stayed and on both sides of the sea, an anger was smoldering that would turn those of Gaelic descent to rebellion against the Crown once again.

By the 1850s, McGrath cottages stood hollow in Munster's hills and Ulster's valleys. Entire families had pawned their few possessions. They sold iron pots, chipped plates, the last of their cattle – whatever they had of any value at all for passage aboard the dreaded "coffin ships." The Atlantic was as much a graveyard as a pathway, but for those who survived, new worlds awaited.

The McGraths swarmed into America's great immigrant ports. New York City became the heart of the diaspora, its Five Points and Brooklyn tenements filling with Irish families. From there, they spread inland. Some settled in Boston, others along the Erie Canal toward upstate New York, and many to the growing cities of Chicago and Philadelphia. The work they could get was usually back-breaking but the Irish were toughened by hardship and it was better than starvation.

In America, the Irish refugees were often reviled – at first. Arriving poor, emaciated, unwashed, with strange accents, bawdy music and in large numbers, many Americans referred to the immigrants as the "Dirty Irish." Employment postings often included the words, "No Irish need apply." It was not an easy transition and the mean streets of America's urban centers were not paved with gold!

In time, though, the McGrath name, along with many many other Irish clans would be found in union halls, police precincts, and city politics, woven into the fabric of American life.

In Canada, many McGraths landed at Grosse Île in Quebec, a quarantine station where many perished of typhus before ever reaching the mainland. From there, the survivors pushed westward once cleared. McGraths settled in Montreal and Toronto, taking work in railroads and mills, but also in farming communities along the St. Lawrence Valley and Ontario's new frontiers. Here, the memory of famine remained sharp, and the ties to the old country were fiercely kept.

Farther still, ships carried McGraths to Australia, many arriving in Sydney or Melbourne. Some were "assisted migrants," their passage sponsored by colonial schemes desperate for labor. Others had already arrived as convicts, as Australia was used as a British penal colony, but later immigrants arrived as free settlers chasing gold in the Victorian goldfields. In the Australian bush, McGraths became stockmen, farmers, and miners, carrying with them songs of Clare and Thomond to a land down under and utterly foreign.

What united them all, whether in the crowded streets of New York, the frostbitten farms of Ontario, or the blazing sun of New South Wales, was the same woeful tale. They were people driven by hunger, torn from the shadow of castles and bardic schools that had once marked their clan's greatness, now forced to build anew. The McGrath name endured, carried in accents that softened over generations but always held a trace of Ireland's sorrow and stubborn pride. Many kept close ties to their homeland and would soon contribute from across the seas to the next battle for Irish independence against the British Crown.

50

The McGraths Reach America

The Potato Famine unquestionably drove the largest exodus of Irish to America, but there were of course, earlier Irish-Americans. Arthur Magrath, for example is recorded as receiving land in Charleston, South Carolina district as early the 1760s. Andrew Gordon Magrath (1813-1893) who was likely a descendant of Arthur later became governor of South Carolina.

Muster rolls from New York regiments during the war of 1812 include a Patrick McGrath, who had arrived in the early nineteenth century. He represents an earlier wave of working-class Irish Catholics entering northern U.S. cities before the famine. Men bearing the name Patrick seem to tend toward a fighting spirit, as there are several Patrick McGraths who appear in the annals of battle, rebellion and military enlistment – you'll notice several are mentioned throughout this book!

Passenger lists kept in New York (mandatory from 1820) also document some early McGrath arrivals in the New World. Edward McGrath (Charleston, 1802), Richard McGrath (Philadelphia, 1806), and James McGrath (New York, 1811) are among the first found in official pre-famine immigration records. These individuals often came as single men, sometimes indentured, and found work in construction, dock labor, or as soldiers.

The influx of McGraths to the US ramped up with the Irish famine, beginning in 1845. Many of these immigrants arrived with very little money, few possessions, limited prospects and tended to concentrate into the kinds of work that required hard labor more than formal training. As a result, little is known about their individual lives but thousands of Irish immigrants worked on the Erie Canal, the Illinois & Michigan Canal, and the rapidly expanding rail networks of the 1840s-50s. Irishmen were also a major presence on the wharves of New York, Boston, and Philadelphia, unloading cargo, driving carts, and hauling goods.

The Irish were also known for stonework. Bricklaying, digging foundations, quarrying stone, masonry. Irish hands built much of the infrastructure of America's growing cities in the Nineteenth Century.

Irish women also found employment where they could. They were overwhelmingly employed as servants in middle and upper-class households, particularly in Boston and New York. Others found work cooking, doing laundry, cleaning, and childcare. For many Irish women, this was the most stable path to survival in America.

Most McGraths who came to America to escape famine led simple lives, content with earning a living and raising families, some of those refugees did rise to prominence and are remembered by history.

In keeping with clan tradition, Mary Elizabeth McGrath - Blake (1840-1907) was renowned for her words. A Waterford McGrath, Mary Elizabeth emigrated with her family in 1849 and became a recognized poet and travel writer in the United States.

John W. McGrath (1842-1895) was elected to the Michigan Supreme Court in the 1890s – a very high distinction indeed for an Irish immigrant of the time.

Another Waterford McGrath named Thomas is remembered for his military service. Thousands of Irish immigrants enlisted for military service, but while the US army was always hungry for warm bodies, the Irish were generally segregated. Thomas McGrath was one example of an early member of the famous Irish Brigade. The Irish saw military service as both a means to obtain steady pay and to prove their loyalty to their adopted country and it had an impact.

By the late nineteenth century, Irish names filled the rolls of city police departments and firehouses. In New York, precinct houses echoed with Gaelic accents, and in Boston, Irish firefighters risked their lives in a city that had once sneered at them as outsiders. These roles became stepping stones to political power. Police and fire departments were not only livelihoods but networks of influence; they connected Irish men to ward bosses, parishes, and political machines that would propel their sons and grandsons into city halls and statehouses. What likely began as desperation for employment – taking the jobs no one else wanted – grew into a legacy of service and civic leadership. In short order, the sight of an Irishman in uniform was no longer an oddity but a tradition.

One heroic example was famine-immigrant Daniel McGrath who rose through the ranks to become chief of police in In the normally quiet streets of Titusville, Pennsylvania. Daniel had spent sixteen years serving his community until, on a cold November day in 1899, he and a fellow officer responded to a burglary at the railroad depot. Arriving at the scene, the situation erupted into a deadly shootout. McGrath faced the danger head-on, exchanging fire with the robbers, and in the chaos, he was mortally wounded.

His death would not be in vain, however. One suspect was killed in the exchange, and the other faced justice in a court of law. McGrath's grave in St. Catherine's Cemetery became more than a final resting place. It remains a marker of Irish-American dedication and sacrifice. From the rough streets of New York and Boston to towns like Titusville, Irish immigrants had transformed from outsiders into the backbone of police and fire services.

Badges and helmets now worn by many bearing the McGrath name were a shining symbol of a down-and-out clan back on the rise in a new land.

In the Army Now

The morning mist hung over the New York harbor as dozens of young Irishmen gathered at the enlistment office, their eyes scanning the docked transports and the gray waters beyond. They spoke in the lilting brogues of Dublin, Cork, and Kilkenny, laughter mingling with the nervous murmurs of first-time soldiers.

Recruiters in blue uniforms handed out papers and polished buttons, but the men weren't here merely for pay. They were here to serve with their own, to fight shoulder to shoulder with those who shared their language, their faith, and the memory of a homeland still aching under British rule. But they also came to prove their loyalty and worth to a new country who hadn't exactly welcomed them with open arms. It could be said the huge waves of Irish immigrants during the famine years were barely tolerated, but that would soon change.

The Irish Brigade was born in the first summer of the American Civil War, when the Union called for volunteers and the streets of New York echoed with drums, cheers, and the shuffle of immigrant steps. Out of that energy rose Brigadier General Thomas Francis Meagher, a man whose life itself was a saga. Meagher had been a revolutionary in Ireland, a leader of the failed Young Ireland Rising of 1848, who had been sentenced to death by the British, exiled to Tasmania, and eventually escaped to America. By 1861 he was living in New York, a lawyer, orator, and symbol of defiance. When the war broke out, he saw a chance for the Irish in America to prove their loyalty to their adopted homeland, and perhaps to hone the martial skills and spirit that might one day help liberate Ireland itself.

From the beginning, the Irish Brigade was more than a military unit. It was a brotherhood of immigrants who had faced hunger, prejudice, and back-breaking work. Most of them had fled the potato famine only a decade earlier. In the slums of New York, Boston, and Philadelphia, they were mocked in newspapers, barred from work by signs reading "No Irish Need Apply," and branded as "dirty" outsiders. But in the army, they saw an opportunity: steady pay, food, camaraderie, and hopefully, *respect.* By fighting under the Stars and Stripes, they could silence their critics and claim their place in the American story.

Segregating the Irish wasn't exactly official policy of the Army, and some units were mixed, but it served well for recruitment and unit cohesion. Officers and priests walked through parishes and taverns, urging Irishmen to stand together, to march shoulder to shoulder with their countrymen. Enlistment posters promised they would fight in regiments filled with fellow Catholics, led by Irish officers who spoke their language and understood their struggles.

Thus, Meagher's Brigade came together: the 69th New York Infantry, already famous for parading on St. Patrick's Day; the 63rd and 88th New York Infantry; soon joined by the 28th Massachusetts and the 116th Pennsylvania formed the Irish Brigade. When they marched, they carried not just the Union flag but also a brilliant green banner embroidered with a golden harp of Erin, the symbol of Ireland itself. The harp gleamed under the sun, flanked with the mottos "Who Never Retreated from the Clash of Spears," (in Gaelic) and *"Erin Go Bragh,"* meaning

"Ireland Forever." The men marched into battle beneath both flags. One for their new nation, one for their ancestral home.

At Antietam, Fredericksburg, Gettysburg, and beyond, they fought with a fury born of memory and hope. They left thousands of Irish names carved into the stone of history and written in blood on America's battlefields.

Naturally, there were many McGraths who served in the Irish Brigade during the American Civil War. One notable example is Captain Eugene McGrath. He was severely wounded at the first battle of Bull Run in July 1861 while attempting to rally his men. Reports indicate that he was run down by Confederate cavalry during the engagement.

After immigrating in 1858, Thomas McGrath of Waterford had initially worked as a baker before enlisting in the Union Army. Thomas served in the Irish Brigade and participated in significant battles, including the particularly famous Battle of Gettysburg. He later shared his experiences in a letter published fifty years after the war.

December 13th, 1862, the winter sun rose pale over Fredericksburg casting long shadows across Marye's Heights. Below, the Confederate lines crouched behind their stone wall, well dug-in and ready for the Union assault. Against impossible odds, the Irish Brigade stepped forward, a mass of blue-coated, musket-wielding men, their hearts pounding with the rhythm of company drummers and centuries of struggle back in Ireland.

At the front waved the green silk banner embroidered with the golden harp of Erin, alongside the Stars and Stripes.

Drums beating, bayonets fixed, the Brigade advanced over frozen ground strewn with mud and debris. Confederate artillery and rifle fire raked the field, cutting down men by the dozens with every step. But the Irish pressed forward, their courage fueled by the voice of their commander, Thomas Francis Meagher, who rode among them, urging, steadying, and inspiring. Each volley they returned, each step forward, was a victory over the prejudice and hardship that had marked their lives in America. It became a charge that would enter legend, a story told and retold in homes and parishes from New York to Boston, of men who dared to storm an impregnable wall with faith, fury, and a courage born of unity. But it ended in tragedy.

The Union assault had failed to break the Confederate lines behind Marye's Heights, and thousands of soldiers lay dead or wounded, their blood soaking into the frozen mud. The Irish Brigade, known as a proud and tightly-knit formation, had suffered horrific casualties. Roughly half of its men were killed, wounded, or missing by the end of the day. The green banner of Erin and the Stars and Stripes, carried so bravely into the storm of bullets, were shredded and bloodied.

Fredericksburg became a crucible in which the Irish identity in America was forged anew, however. Though the field was a bloody testament to the cost of war, it also immortalized the Irish Brigade's courage: men who had once been scorned as outsiders now stood, in the annals of history, as heroes of the Union cause. Their legacy of bravery, loyalty, and pride in heritage would inspire generations of Irish-Americans long after the guns and bugles fell silent.

While the Irish Brigade of New York, Massachusetts, and Pennsylvania is the most famous of the Irish Civil War units, it was only one part of a much larger tapestry of Irish soldiers who fought in the American Civil War.

Regiments such as the 9th Massachusetts Infantry also carried Irish names, traditions, and banners into battle. From the records of the "Fighting Ninth," we find another "fighting" Patrick McGrath among the enlisted.

Various Irish units (often joining with the Irish Brigade) fought in campaigns across Virginia, Maryland, and Pennsylvania, facing brutal engagements at Antietam, Chancellorsville, and Gettysburg. Meanwhile, the 116th Pennsylvania Infantry brought men from Philadelphia's Irish parishes to the front lines, joining the famed Irish Brigade and reinforcing the reputation of Irish soldiers for courage and tenacity.

On the Confederate side, Irish immigrants were no less committed. Units like the 1st Virginia Battalion ("Irish Battalion"), the 10th Tennessee Infantry, and the Louisiana Tigers drew heavily on Irish Catholic communities in the South. These regiments were known for their ferocity and discipline, often thrown into the most dangerous fighting.

Across both armies, Irish soldiers carried symbols of their homeland into battle: shamrocks pinned to caps, green sashes, and the golden harp of Erin on banners. Even as they fought for different American causes, these men, sometimes even fighting members of their own clans, still maintained a kind of unity for the cause of Irish liberation.

The Irish Units serving the Union Army, their numbers tattered by horrific losses at Fredricksburg still pressed on. Regrouping, reorganizing, they were deployed to defend against Confederate encroachment into the North at the Battle of Gettysburg.

In July 1863, the morning sun rose over the rolling hills of Gettysburg, casting long shadows over a landscape soon to be torn apart by smoke, cannon fire, and the cries of clashing men. The green banners of the Irish Brigade again fluttered beside the Stars and Stripes. As the battle erupted, the Irish soldiers advanced into the maelstrom, bayonets fixed, muskets blazing, across fields riddled with artillery fire. At Culp's Hill and the Wheatfield, they faced relentless volleys from Confederate sharpshooters and musket lines. Men fell around them by the dozen. Officers shouted orders over the roar of battle, but the Union Army's discipline and courage were rooted in the streets, parishes, and neighborhoods they were fighting to defend. This was their home territory – the lands that housed their own families. No less so for the Irish and their adopted homes.

Thomas McGrath, who had survived Fredericksburg was again fighting shoulder to shoulder with his comrades in the Irish Brigade. The Fighting Ninth brought Patrick McGrath back into battle at Gettysburg as well. They and countless others fought not only to hold the Union line but to show the world the mettle of the Irish immigrant. By the end of the three-day inferno, casualties were staggering; entire regiments had been decimated, yet their bravery had held key positions and bought precious time for reinforcements to stabilize the front and the Army of the Confederacy was broken. Union losses were dire but for the South, Gettysburg was devastating and a turning point in the US Civil War leading to ultimate victory for preservation of the United States and by extension, the end of human slavery in the South.

When the guns finally fell silent, the Irish soldiers who had marched beneath the green harp banner returned to a nation forever changed. In many ways, so were they. Many had enlisted to prove their loyalty to a country that had so often spurned them, a land that still whispered "No Irish Need Apply" in shop windows and hiring offices. But on the battlefields of Fredericksburg, Antietam, and Gettysburg, they had fought and bled for the Union as fiercely as any who were born in America. When they came home, scarred but ultimately victorious, they carried with them a new sense of belonging. The Irish were no longer just laborers or exiles. They were veterans, citizens who had earned their place in the nation's story with musket and drum.

In the years that followed, Irish veterans helped transform their communities, many taking up work in the city fire brigades or police departments, bringing discipline and heroism honed in war to the protection of their adopted neighborhoods. Others rose into politics, unions, and business.

In Wisconsin, for example, Irish immigrant James McGrath served nine years in the state assembly after the Civil War and Edmond McGrath found success in business in Upstate New York.

Though prejudice lingered, The courage that had been proven in the smoke of battle could not be denied. The war that had divided America had, for the Irish, become the struggle that finally began to unite them with it. But, while many Irish veterans began integrating, thousands would also soon turn their attention back to injustices in Ireland.

The Fenians

After the American Civil War, whispers traveled faster than ships across the gray harbors of green Ireland. They said that men were coming home from America – men who had fought in the great war there, who had seen death and victory, who were trained and battle-hardened and who now spoke of Ireland's freedom with the same fire that had kept them alive on battlefields like Antietam and Gettysburg.

They were called Fenians, after the legendary Fianna warriors of old, and they came armed not only with muskets and sabers, but with the fierce conviction that the time for Irish independence had come. The American Civil War had ended, and its Irish veterans – men who had marched under the green harp banner of the Irish Brigade – now turned their eyes east, across the Atlantic, toward the homeland they had left behind.

In taverns from New York to Boston, and in the smoky back rooms of Dublin and Cork, plans were whispered in Gaelic and English alike.

The Irish Republican Brotherhood (IRB), founded in Ireland a few years earlier in 1858, had grown into a transatlantic conspiracy. Their symbol was the sunburst, their motto simple: *Ireland for the Irish*. And their plan was audacious – an armed uprising across Ireland, fueled by money, weapons, and veterans from America. Their Irish-American allies were named the Fenian

Brotherhood (but the term would later describe the whole movement.

By 1866, Irish-American Fenians gathered along the U.S.-Canadian border, their tattered blue Union jackets still smelling faintly of powder. They marched north, not to defend the United States, but to bring war to the empire that had driven their ancestors to hunger. "We'll take Canada," they said, "and trade it back to Britain for Ireland." The so-called Fenian Raids began – half-mad, half-glorious adventures. At Ridgeway, near Niagara, they clashed with Canadian militia and won a brief, defiant victory. Though the raids ultimately failed, they struck fear into the British government and gave the Irish cause new life.

Then came March of 1867, when the fire leapt back across the sea. In the green hills of Tipperary and the streets of Dublin, Irish rebels rose. They were poorly armed, betrayed by informants, and once again, crushed by British troops – yet their rebellion burned like a spark in the wet kindling of history. The hangings that followed, the Manchester Martyrs and the prisoners in English jails, only deepened the sense that Ireland had once again been wronged but not crushed.

Among the rebels were men who had left Irish soil as boys and returned as soldiers – Patrick McGrath of Clare, Sean O'Leary of Cork, Thomas Clarke Luby, and others whose names would endure through history and lineage. They fought in scattered bands, striking at constables and barracks, hiding in bogs and heathered hills. Some escaped back to America; others met the noose with prayers on their lips and the word "Éire" as their last breath.

But if the rebellion failed in arms, it triumphed in spirit. From its ashes rose a generation of Irish who no longer begged for pity or compromise. The Fenians had proved that the Irish would

never stop fighting for Ireland and that her sons across the ocean
had not forgotten her cry.

The House that Endured

English Plantation policy had systematically stripped Irish Catholic nobles and Gaelic chiefs of their lands, transferring vast estates to English and Scottish Protestant settlers. Most Gaelic lineages – McGrath, O'Brien, O'Neill, and others – were dispossessed, forced into tenancy, exile, or clerical service. However, not all Gaelic families were completely ruined.

In Munster, where the O'Briens had once ruled Thomond, a few branches managed to *bend* without fully breaking. Some converted to Protestantism – at least outwardly – to preserve property or legal standing (it was then illegal for Catholics to own property). Others allied through marriage with Old English families (Catholics of Norman descent) who were permitted to retain portions of their estates. The O'Briens were masters of this strategy: while some members joined rebellions, others entered English service, received titles, and even sat in Parliament.

For the McGraths of Waterford and Clare, these old alliances with the O'Briens remained crucial. When their own lands were seized or reduced, service to their more powerful kin kept them within reach of some influence and protection. Dispossessed McGraths were able to gradually reestablish themselves under the cover of their patrons' name.

For centuries, the O'Briens walked a careful path, outwardly loyal to the Crown yet inwardly true to their Irish heritage. In that fraught shadow, the McGraths endured. They continued on as parish priests and tutors, preserving both faith and history through the long winter of English rule. When the Penal Laws descended in the eighteenth century, barring Catholics from owning land or holding office, the McGraths held fast, passing their lineage quietly from father to son in humble cottages along the River Fergus.

Then came the Famine. Ireland's fields starved under blight, and millions were driven to exile or death. Yet amid that tragedy, a strange turn of fortune began. As Ireland's population collapsed, many of the planted English landlords began to feel the pinch, as well. Crippled by debt and depopulation, they began to sell their estates. For the first time in generations, Irish Catholic families – educated, industrious, and determined – could reclaim the soil that had once been theirs.

Among them was William Henry McGrath of Toonagh, born in the shadow of loss but driven by the hunger to restore his family's place in Clare. He was a man of learning, a descendant of poets turned pragmatist, whose education and quiet resolve won him respect in both Catholic and Protestant circles. In 1852, he married Bridget O'Brien of Birchfield, herself descended from Cennétig's noble line that had weathered centuries of confiscation and compromise.

The O'Briens of Birchfield were a landed Catholic family of some means who had survived the worst of the penal era, in part by keeping a low profile and maintaining good relations with Protestant gentry. When Bridget O'Brien married William Henry McGrath, it wasn't just a family union – it was a consolidation of two Dál gCais lines that had managed to thread the needle between persecution and prosperity. Their marriage gave the McGraths access to Birchfield influence, while the O'Briens gained an educated and ambitious ally. It was the rekindling of an ancient alliance.

The McGraths had once chronicled the deeds of the O'Briens; now the two families stood together again, not as masters and bards, but as equals. With the easing of the Penal Laws and the decline of the old Anglo-Irish estates, William Henry seized his chance. Bit by bit, through shrewd management and well-timed acquisitions, he built an estate of 3,000 acres, restoring the McGrath name to prominence in Ireland for the first time since the fall of Gaelic rule.

The Uncrowned King

When the smoke of the Fenian uprisings faded, Ireland seemed quiet – but it was the kind of quiet that hides the heartbeat of a plot. The people were weary, the rebels scattered, the prisons full. Yet, in that silence, something remarkable was happening. Across the western farmlands, from Mayo to Clare, tenants whispered not of guns but of justice – of the soil beneath their feet and the alien landlords who claimed it as their own.

It was a different kind of revolution now, and its champion was a one-armed veteran named Michael Davitt, himself a child of famine and eviction. In 1879, he founded the Irish National Land League, a movement that would shake the very foundations of British rule – not with gunfire, but with boycotts, strikes, and moral courage. "The land of Ireland for the people of Ireland," Davitt declared, and for the first time, the phrase was more than a dream.

Where the Fenians had fought with rifles, the Land Leaguers fought with rent strikes. They refused to pay unjust landlords. They banded together in secret councils. When an agent tried to seize a tenant's crop, the whole parish might rise as one to block his way. The very word "boycott" was born from these battles, named for Captain Charles Boycott, whose estate was shunned so completely that he eventually had to import workers from Ulster under armed guard to keep his besieged estate operating.

Leaders of the Land League had observed generations of crushing defeats when the Irish staged armed uprising, so now they preached restraint. They adopted the tactics of the McGraths, drawing on lessons from history, using the power of words, of laws and politics. Fenian blood still ran in the movement's veins, but many of those same rebels – or their sons – now wore suits instead of uniforms, speaking in Parliament or writing pamphlets instead of rallying in the hills. Among them were McGraths, O'Briens, O'Sullivans, and Murphys, men whose fathers had once fought or died for freedom.

Then came Charles Stewart Parnell, the "Uncrowned King of Ireland," who took the energy of the Land League and transformed it into a political storm. Under his leadership, the Irish Parliamentary Party brought the cause of Home Rule (self-government within the British Empire) into the halls of Westminster. He was polished where the Fenians had been fierce, a master of rhetoric instead of rebellion, but the goal was the same: an Ireland governed by her own people.

From New York and Boston, Irish loyalists poured gold and silver into the movement – money earned by famine refugees who now worked as policemen, firemen, and builders in the New World. Irish-American newspapers printed Parnell's speeches beside stories of eviction and hunger. The Atlantic itself became a bridge of rebellion, each tide carrying sympathy, songs, and silver back to the old country.

By the 1880s, the fight for Ireland had taken on a new shape. The musket had given way to the ballot, and the barricade to the parliamentary bench. But the flame that burned in the Fenians' hearts still glowed – for now tempered, patient, and enduring.

As one old Fenian was said to remark, watching the Land Leaguers march under their green banners:

"We traded our rifles for speeches, but make no mistake. The war goes on."

In the smoky chambers of Westminster, where Irish voices were long drowned beneath the thunder of empire, one man would not be silenced. The "Uncrowned King of Ireland," Charles Stewart Parnell – tall, cold-eyed, and commanding – raised hell in British politics like a ghost out of Ireland's wounded heart. He was part landlord, part rebel and wholly unyielding.

Born in 1846 into the Anglo-Irish gentry, Parnell could easily have lived a quiet, privileged life on his estate in Wicklow. But famine had scarred the land of his childhood, and his mother, a fierce American with revolutionary blood, whispered freedom into his ear from the cradle. By the 1870s, Ireland was restless again. Tenant farmers still toiled on soil they did not own. The Land League, led by fiery men like Michael Davitt, called for fair rent, freedom to buy the land they worked and permanency of landholding rights. What they lacked was a voice that could sway Parliament from within.

Parnell gave them that voice – calm, precise, and devastating. He turned obstruction into a weapon, filibustering the House of Commons for days at a time, forcing the English press and public to hear the Irish cry for justice. His charisma was icy but magnetic, his discipline unbreakable. Even his enemies, hard men committed to empire and conquest, found themselves compelled to respect him.

When Parnell spoke, Ireland listened. When he paused, the world waited.

Under his leadership, the Irish Parliamentary Party rose to become a machine of iron unity. He held it together by sheer force of will, turning a squabbling band of Ministers of Parliament into a disciplined army for Home Rule – If they could not win true independence, the Irish turned to dreams of self-government within the British Empire. By the mid-1880s, that goal seemed within reach. The great William Ewart Gladstone, Prime Minister of Britain, had been converted to the cause. A bill for Irish Home Rule stood before Parliament, and Ireland held its breath.

Then came the scandal.

Parnell's own strong head became his undoing. His long affair with Katharine O'Shea, the wife of one of his own Ministers of Parliament, had been an open secret in political circles. But when Mrs. O'Shea's husband filed for divorce in 1890, the sordid details were splashed across every newspaper in Britain. The revelation shocked Victorian society and split the Irish movement in two. Priests denounced him from their pulpits. Former allies turned their backs.

Parnell refused to yield. He declared that no English moral code would dictate the destiny of Ireland. But the tide had turned. His health failed under the weight of scandal and betrayal. In 1891, at only forty-five years old, Charles Stewart Parnell died in the arms of Katharine, worn down by the battle he had taken charge of but would not live to see won. When word of his demise reached Ireland, thousands wept openly in the streets.

A statue of Parnell in Dublin now bears his famous words:

"No man has a right to fix the boundary of the march of a nation."

Parnell's public decline and death was a grievous blow to Irish hopes, yet his fall did not end the struggle; it transformed it. The generation that followed – men like Padraig Pearse, James Connolly, and Éamon de Valera – grew up under the shadow of Parnell's ghost. They saw that moral appeals and parliamentary patience could only go so far. The failure of Home Rule fanned the smoldering ember of rebellion back into a blaze.

When gunfire returned to the streets of Dublin in 1916, they echoed the words Parnell had once spoken: that a nation must stand on its own feet, and bow to no one. His tragedy became Ireland's resolve. The Uncrowned King had fallen, but the kingdom he dreamed of was coming.

Our Day Will Come

In the summer of 1914, the world stumbled into madness. The assassination of an archduke in Sarajevo – a single spark in a Balkan backwater – ignited a fire that swept across Europe. Bound by treaties and pride, Britain found itself drawn into what would first become the Great War (later known as World War I), a conflict unlike anything the world had ever seen. Men marched off by the millions, believing it would be over by Christmas. It was not. By the time the trenches clawed through Flanders and the Somme, the war had devoured a generation.

In Ireland, the call to arms came heavy with contradiction. The British government promised that once Germany was defeated, Home Rule for Ireland, long delayed, would finally be granted. Tens of thousands of Irishmen enlisted, some out of loyalty to the Crown, but many others out of hope that their sacrifice would buy freedom for Ireland. Yet as Irish blood soaked the fields of Belgium and France, the chains of empire held fast. For many at home in Ireland, the war felt less like a cause and more like a colossal lie.

It was in this shadow, while the world tore itself apart, that Ireland's own destiny stirred.

The British Empire, distracted and weakened by the global struggle, had left its garrison in Dublin thin and complacent. The moment was ripe, and a handful of visionaries seized it. Patrick

Pearse, James Connolly, Thomas Clarke, and their comrades in the Irish Republican Brotherhood and Irish Volunteers believed the war had created a divine opportunity: England's difficulty was opportunity for Ireland.

In the spring of 1916, Ireland burned – not with fire alone, but with a passion for freedom.

The British Empire, locked in the bloodbath of the Great War, had conscripted Irishmen by the tens of thousands to die on foreign soil. Yet in the heart of Dublin, a small band of dreamers decided that their blood would be shed for Ireland instead.

They were poets, teachers, clerks and farmers – the kind of men no empire expects to fear. Patrick Pearse, the schoolmaster who spoke like a prophet; James Connolly, the socialist firebrand; Thomas Clarke, the old Fenian who had waited a lifetime for this day. And behind them stood the Irish Republican Brotherhood, that old secret network born in the smoky rooms of Dublin and Boston alike, sworn to one cause: *Ireland for the Irish*.

At noon on Easter Monday, April 24th, 1916, they seized Dublin's General Post Office and raised a strange new flag – green, white, and orange – declaring an Irish Republic in the name of God and generations who had suffered and died under British rule. The flag design had actually existed much longer, being presented to Brigadier General Thomas Francis Meagher of the Young Irish Rebellion of 1848 by a small group of French women sympathetic to the cause of Irish liberty. The flag design was a symbol of hope for peace and unity between the Irish Catholics (symbolized by the green) and the Anglo Protestants (orange), with the white band between representing a lasting truce, but that Easter was the first time the flag was raised in the name of an Irish Republic.

For six days, they fought against overwhelming odds, outgunned and surrounded by British troops and artillery. When the smoke cleared, much of Dublin lay in ruins. Yet another Irish rebellion had failed.

Or so the British thought.

The executions that followed – one by one, in the cold gray dawn transformed martyrs into legends. The Irish people, weary and divided, again united with a forceful new conviction. Across the countryside, whispers spread in the Gaelic tongue: *"The fight is not over."*

Among the young men who took up that conviction were veterans of the Irish Volunteers, who reorganized quietly in the years after the crushed Rising. In small country parishes, in pubs and back rooms, they began drilling again, using whatever weapons they could find. One such group met regularly in County Tipperary, where the names of their leaders – Séamus Robinson, Seán Treacy, Dan Breen – would soon echo through history.

And among them, in Ulster, Patrick McGrath, a Volunteer organizer from Donegal, kept the embers alive. A descendant of the old McGraths of Termonmagrath, Patrick served as a courier and intelligence man for the Republican cause. He ferried messages, weapons, and men through the northern counties, working under the radar of British authorities who had long suspected the McGraths of nationalist sympathies. His role was quiet but vital, one of many invisible threads that bound together Ireland's rising tide of resistance.

By 1919, that tide broke hard against the embankments of British Power.

On January 21st, the first *Dáil Éireann*, a revolutionary Irish Parliament, convened in Dublin and declared independence. That same day, members of the Irish Volunteers ambushed a Royal Irish Constabulary convoy at Soloheadbeg, killing two officers and seizing their weapons. It was the first military engagement of the Irish War of Independence. The attackers did not yet know it, but the confluence of events had just given birth to a new name for an old dream: the Irish Republican Army – *Óglaigh na hÉireann*.

Under Michael Collins, the IRA became more than an underground movement. It became an organized fighting force. Collins, the young Corkman with a mind like lightning, transformed unrest into organization. He built networks of spies in Dublin Castle, hit squads in the streets, and flying columns in the countryside. The war that followed was not akin to the one fought in Europe. It was a crafty war of shadows, whispers, ambushes and reprisals. Instead of trenches, it was fought in alleys, public houses and government buildings.

The IRA, forged from the ashes of Pearse's rebellion, struck with cunning precision, hitting police barracks, convoys, and informants. Every success carried the echo of the men of 1916, the ghost of the tricolor flag that had briefly flown above the Dublin Post Office.

And behind it all, families like the McGraths – teachers, priests, messengers, and soldiers – sustained the movement. Some carried rifles; others carried bread, letters, or stretchers bearing wounded. In Donegal, Limerick, and Clare, they offered safehouses and local knowledge. Bards who would have once chronicled kings now chronicled a new kind of hero: the freedom fighter.

By 1921, England and Ireland had bled enough. The Anglo-Irish Treaty, signed in December, offered a measure of self-government: it created the Irish Free State, a dominion within the British Empire with its own parliament and control over domestic affairs. But the treaty also required an oath of allegiance to the Crown, and it allowed six northern counties to remain under British rule – the partition that created Northern Ireland. The island was divided; the struggle for a fully independent republic, as Patrick Pearse had dreamed, was unfinished. Yet even in the bitter peace that followed, one truth remained: the IRA had risen from the ruins of the Easter Rising to become the living embodiment of Ireland's defiant soul, its legacy echoing in every field, street, and heart that still longed for freedom.

And as the veterans of 1916 were laid to rest, a new generation stood ready, proudly lamenting, *"Ní bheidh ár leithéidí ann arís."* – *We will not see their like again.*

The ink was barely dry on the Anglo-Irish Treaty of December 1921 when the sound of celebration began to curdle into the murmur of dissent. The agreement, signed between British representatives and Irish delegates led by Michael Collins and Arthur Griffith, had promised an end to centuries of bloodshed, but at a cost. Ireland would become a Free State, yes, with its own parliament and dominion status within the British Commonwealth. But it would not be the republic that men like Pádraig Pearse had died for. Worse still, six counties in the north – Antrim, Armagh, Down, Fermanagh, Londonderry (Preferentially known as Derry by Irish nationalists), and Tyrone – were to remain under British rule as Northern Ireland. The island was split, the tricolor itself seeming to tear at the seams.

Many in Ireland hailed the treaty as a victory, a first step toward full freedom. Collins himself famously called it "the freedom to achieve freedom." Yet others saw it as a betrayal. Éamon de Valera, who had served as President of the *Dáil Éireann* during the war, refused to accept the oath of allegiance the treaty demanded to the British Crown. The IRA, once united in defiance, fractured into pro-Treaty and anti-Treaty factions, brother now turning against brother.

By 1922, the tension broke into open conflict: the Irish Civil War. Collins, then leading the new provisional government, found himself fighting the very men who had stood shoulder to shoulder with him against the British. The battle lines were drawn in Dublin itself: the anti-Treaty forces, under Rory O'Connor, occupied the Four Courts, defying the new government's authority. When the Free State forces, armed with British artillery, shelled the building in June, the struggle for independence from England transformed overnight into a war among the Irish themselves.

Across the island, families were divided by loyalty and conscience. In Tipperary, Liam McGrath, a former IRA courier turned anti-Treaty fighter, was said to have lamented before his execution, "We fought the Empire, and now we're tearing at our own heart." The civil war was cruel, chaotic, and deeply personal. Michael Collins himself was killed in an ambush in his native Cork in August 1922, a tragic symbol of Ireland's self-inflicted wound.

By May 1923, the Anti-Treaty forces, exhausted and demoralized, laid down their arms. The Free State survived – but the unity that had bound Ireland in rebellion lay shattered. In every parish and town, scars remained: friendships ended, graves multiplied, and a nation's dream of freedom was shadowed by grief. Yet from that turmoil emerged the political divide that would shape Ireland for generations – Fianna Fáil and Fine Gael, born from the two opposing sides of the Treaty's promise and its price. In the end, Ireland remained divided into North and South and the new border also split apart Clan McGrath.

An Island and a Clan Divided

When the Anglo-Irish Treaty of 1921 drew a line between the new Irish Free State and Northern Ireland, it did not merely divide geography – it cut through kinship, history, and memory. For the McGraths, whose lineage reached back as Ulster's ancient ecclesiastical keepers and poets, the border came like a fresh wound – one that divided a clan and its loyalties.

In County Donegal, a McGrath heartland that had once been firmly part of Gaelic Ulster, the new border isolated them. Donegal found itself awkwardly inside the Free State, but barely. Donegal actually sits farther north than Northern Ireland. The neighboring counties of Tyrone and Fermanagh, to the southeast, also traditionally McGrath territory, were locked within British-controlled Northern Ireland. Families who had attended the same markets in Pettigo or worshiped together at Lough Derg now needed papers or courage to cross what became a heavily patrolled border. Pettigo itself – that ancient pilgrimage town where McGraths, O'Donnels, Maguires and O'Faheys mingled for centuries – was literally split in two. In 1922, it became a flashpoint of armed conflict between Free State troops and the Ulster Special Constabulary, as the new border was contested in blood.

In the twilight of 1921, Ireland had seemed poised on the edge of something new. There had been hope for peace – the promise represented by the tricolor flag. The signing of the Anglo-Irish Treaty granted a measure of independence, yet the fresh wound of a hard border dividing the island was repugnant to Gaelic loyalists and it would not be accepted easily.

For McGraths rooted in Ulster, in places like Fermanagh and Donegal, the border was not just a political line on a map – it was a fracture in family, land, and memory. Across that new frontier, the McGrath name which had once marked poets and hereditary church-guardians now stood amid suspicion, surveillance, and divided loyalties.

Some McGraths of Fermanagh and Tyrone stayed loyal to the republican cause, smuggling weapons and supplies across the border into the Free State. Others, wary of reprisals or economic ruin, sought work under the new Northern administration, blending reluctantly into a system they did not recognize as their own. The division also encouraged a new wave of emigration: younger McGraths from both sides of the line left for America, Liverpool, and Australia rather than live in a fractured homeland.

The McGraths of the North found themselves living as part of a Catholic minority, or as borderland families whose land, livelihood and identity were caught in the shadow of partition.

Thomas was an Ulster McGrath, who, himself found himself on the wrong side of the new British border. Born in 1891 in County Fermanagh, deep in the borderlands of the newly declared Northern Ireland, he remained a republican loyalist and when the border was still a fresh wound, he began work that would earn him the name, "Border Ghost."

To the British officers who patrolled the new customs posts, Tom was just another cattle dealer from Fermanagh – quiet, forgettable. He'd rumble by them with a cart loaded with hay or turf. But beneath the bundles, tucked in false compartments and hidden under the seat boards, he carried messages, weapons, and money – the invisible threads binding republicans on both sides of the border together.

He had fought before, though not in any glorious way. During the War of Independence, Tom had served as a courier and organizer – one of the countless "unknown soldiers" who never wore medals or took public credit. He was too wary of fame, too deliberate for martyrdom. The men in Dublin called him "the Border Ghost," because he was everywhere and nowhere at once, slipping across checkpoints with the same quiet ease as the mist over Lough Erne.

When the Anglo-Irish Treaty carved the island in two, Tom didn't pick up his rifle again. He had seen enough killing. But he didn't stop fighting, either. His war became one of whispers and wires, not bullets – a war of smuggled correspondence, secret meetings in barns, and coded telegrams to Irish-American contacts still funneling cash to the cause.

By the mid-1930s, the Free State government was consolidating, and the IRA's northern brigades were starving for leadership. Tom was already a veteran in his forties, his hair gone grey, but he returned to the field with quiet resolve. He knew the borderland terrain like the veins on his hand. There were nights when he guided young idealists through the hedgerows toward Donegal, teaching them where to step, when to freeze, how to vanish. To them he seemed almost mythical – a relic of the old war who still believed unity was possible and who knew how to both fight and survive in the meantime.

The Royal Ulster Constabulary had his name. So did the Free State's intelligence bureau. But Tom McGrath had long since learned that survival depended on invisibility. He never gave speeches or posed for photographs. He didn't write memoirs or make boasts in pubs. Yet, when the history of that uneasy decade is reviewed – through intercepted letters, smuggled arms, and the reawakening of republican cells along the northern frontier – Tom McGrath's fingerprints appear like faint echoes of a man who refused to let the line on the map become a scar on the heard of Ireland.

Meanwhile, in Waterford and Tipperary, branches of the family who had been long established in Gaelic society thrived again under Free State, seeing themselves as part of a reborn Gaelic nation. They took pride in Ireland's new institutions – its schools, civil service, and army – while watching with unease as their northern cousins endured decades of sectarian tension.

In the Free State, Joseph McGrath – a Dublin-born McGrath who had fought in the Rising and the War of Independence, rose swiftly through the new government's ranks.

Born into Rutledge Terrace in the heart of the Irish capital, Joe had grown up selling newspapers on street corners, eager for a life beyond the narrow lanes and drab tenements. His friends at the accounting firm Craig Gardiner & Co. included a bright-eyed clerk named Michael Collins; together they slipped into the secret world of the Irish Republican Brotherhood, pledging their names in the quiet nights. When the Easter Rising erupted, McGrath fought in the ranks at Marrowbone Lane, saw comrades fall, and tasted the bitter cost of revolution.

After the war of independence, when Ireland was carved apart by the Treaty and the Civil War raged, Joe McGrath took another mantle: government minister. At just 34 years old, in January 1922 he became Minister for Labour in the new Free State; by August he held the post of Minister for Industry and Commerce. His success marked a shift for the McGrath name – from the margins of a repressed Gaelic society back into the corridors of power in the new Ireland.

But the promise of unity had already cracked. As Free State and anti-Treaty forces turned on each other in the Irish Civil War,

Joseph found himself Director of Intelligence for the new government's forces. His role entrenched one reality for the McGraths of the era: the family no longer simply stood in opposition to empire – it now had to navigate internal division, statehood, and the cost of compromise.

Through the restless 1920s, the McGrath branches north and south took diverging paths. In the Free State south, many McGraths embraced their place in building the new nation: re-entering politics, business, education, and civil service. In the north, the McGraths were split between continuing the fight for the whole of Ireland, and acquiescing to British rule.

By the mid-1930s, Ireland had settled into its uneasy peace. The Free State now called itself Éire under the 1937 Constitution, while Northern Ireland continued under British rule. For the McGraths, the era had done more than divide land – it had fractured clans and national identity.

Guns for Whiskey

The sea was always the first barrier. Tom McGrath knew it better than most. For the Border Ghost, the Atlantic was more than water – it was a sieve of customs officers, a gauntlet of Coast Guard cutters, a blur of fog and moonlight where fortunes and lives could vanish in hours. By the mid-1920s, the IRA had learned that the struggle at home in Ireland required more than courage and courage alone – it required guns, money, and networks that stretched across oceans.

Tom's task was delicate: He treated with America's Irish underworld in a maze of Irish-American republican networks, speakeasies and bootleggers. Despite Prohibition, Whiskey flowed illegally through Boston and New York like blood through veins, and where there was a demand for liquor, there was opportunity. McGrath and his comrades arranged deals with Irish-American gangsters – men whose hands were as skilled in smuggling barrels as in handling tommy guns – to trade cases of Irish whiskey for cash, for weapons, for both. Every shipment that left an American port carried risk: if discovered, it meant arrest, seizure, or worse. Yet every shipment that succeeded meant rifles for the Free State border, pistols for Belfast, and funds to keep the IRA alive in a country divided by treaties and old loyalties.

In Tom's eyes, he wasn't dealing in a criminal enterprise with gangsters. They were temporary allies in a larger war. He wrote coded letters to colleagues back in Fermanagh, instructing them where shipments would land and which safe houses to secure. Maps drawn on napkins showed rivers, train lines, and hidden coves – a network of surreptitious trade threaded through both Ireland and America.

When the cargo finally reached Ireland, often disguised in shipments of hay or agricultural equipment, McGrath's heart would race. The rifles hidden in false compartments, the barrels of cash tucked beneath sacks of grain – all were lifelines for men and women committed to a vision of Ireland, unified. All could get him killed if discovered.

By the late 1920s, these operations had secured an unbroken flow of weapons and funds, feeding republican units from Ulster to the Free State's northern borders. McGrath's work across the Atlantic never appeared in newspapers; it was a war waged in shadow, whispered in pubs, and remembered in letters folded and hidden for decades. And though history might not name every operative, the barrels of whiskey and the crates of rifles carried by the Atlantic currents bore witness to Tom McGrath's quiet but crucial orchestration of an international struggle for Irish freedom.

As the 1920s wore on, the net tightened. U.S. federal agencies grew savvier, Canada introduced stricter transshipment checks, and Irish ports installed more vigilant customs staff. A number of shipments were intercepted; men were arrested in Boston and London; some were jailed, others deported. Yet the exchanges between the IRA and the US Irish underworld never fully stopped. The old routes hardened into new networks: legal charities and diaspora fundraising replaced some of the crude whiskey-for-guns exchanges; clandestine arms purchases shifted to Europe for concealment; and in Ireland the movement learned

to make its own weapons when foreign sources grew too
dangerous.

86

The Big Guy

While the Border Ghost, Tom McGrath worked the shadows of the partition in Ireland, Edward "Eddie" McGrath was growing a shadowy operation of his own in America. Known on the New York waterfront as "The Big Guy," he wasn't the kind of Irishman who wrote poetry about freedom or sang rebel songs in smoky pubs. His rebellion came in the form of muscle, money, and control.

Eddie was American-born to Irish immigrants in 1906 and grew up in the Gas House District of Manhattan's lower east side. He had a stable upbringing by Catholic parents, served as an alter boy and sang in the choir at St. Steven's Church. Dropping out of high school in tenth grade to work as an office clerk, he later got a job as a truck driver, but as he grew into adulthood, his life took a turn.

In the 1920s and 30s, he was arrested several times on charges ranging from burglary to murder and wound up serving a lengthy stay in Sing Sing prison. After he was released, Eddie became a union organizer for the International Longshoreman's Association on the docks of Hell's Kitchen's waterfront.

The docks along the Hudson weren't just a workplace – they were an open field of opportunity for those bold enough to seize it.

By the 1930s, Alcohol Prohibition had made gangsters into kings. While Italian families like the Genoveses were expanding their reach on the streets and in Speakeasys, the Irish still ruled the docks. Eddie, sharp-eyed and deceptively calm, had begun as a longshoreman – hauling cargo, making friends, taking notes. He learned quickly that everything that came through the piers was worth something to someone. He also learned that fear was currency. When corrupt union officials and petty crooks clashed, McGrath stepped in as peacemaker… and enforcer. His charisma was quiet but effective. Before long, everyone on the West Side waterfront answered to The Big Guy.

McGrath became the primary muscle on the waterfront, with gangsters like John "Cockeye" Dunn (who was Eddie's brother-in-law) and Andrew "Squint" Sheridan as his enforcers. He became a close ally of powerful organized crime figures such as Joe Adonis and Meyer Lansky.

While the Big Guy was never documented as providing direct assistance to the IRA, in general, the Irish Mob in America were known supporters of the cause and shady shipments to or from Ireland on Eddie's docks at least got his nod.

During World War II, The Big Guy's empire flourished. Ships loaded with military supplies docked daily, and the flow of cargo was relentless. Where there was movement, there was money – and McGrath knew how to take his cut without leaving fingerprints. He ran the International Longshoremen's Association (ILA) through a mix of bribes and intimidation, ensuring the waterfront stayed under his command. When rivals emerged – especially those backed by the Italians – McGrath didn't flinch. He partnered with Albert Anastasia, one of the most feared Mafia bosses in America, and forged an unholy alliance between the Irish and Italian mobs. Together, they turned the Manhattan docks into a fortress of organized crime.

But power, like the tide, doesn't stay high forever. In the 1950s, law enforcement turned its gaze to the docks and Eddie's empire began to crack. His close lieutenants, "Cockeye" Dunn and Squint Sheridan were tried and executed for murder and that led to the formation of The Waterfront Commission of New York Harbor to root out corruption. Suddenly, The Big Guy's quiet deals were making headlines. Congressional hearings followed. Friends turned. McGrath, ever pragmatic, sensed the changing winds. Before the hammer could fall, he slipped away, quietly leaving the docks he had ruled for two decades. Some said he retired to Florida, living comfortably off his hidden fortunes. Others whispered that he still pulled strings from the shadows, advising a new generation of mobsters who never knew his name but still followed his rules.

Eddie McGrath's legacy wasn't in politics, poetry or freedom-fighting. It was in the cold mist of the docks at dawn, in the sound of chains rattling and deals whispered, in the empire he built with fists and fear. And even now, on the old piers of Manhattan, they still tell stories about The Big Guy, the Irishman who ruled the waterfront.

Eddie died in 1994 at the age of 88 – in Florida.

The Emergency

Ireland stood like a lone stone cottage on the edge of a world-wide hurricane. Europe had descended into the Second World War, but Ireland's Executive President, Éamon de Valera stood steady, stubborn, and unyielding. He held fast to a policy of Irish neutrality in a period the Irish remember as "The Emergency." The country was poor, its defenses meager, but neutrality became a statement of sovereignty and self-determination. After centuries of English rule, Ireland would now choose its own destiny, even if that meant standing apart from a war many felt sympathetic toward.

Not everyone agreed with the government. Ireland may have officially committed to neutrality, but tens of thousands of Irish men and women nonetheless stepped directly into the global conflict. Some joined the British armed forces, driven by a mix of economic need, family tradition, anti-fascist conviction, or simply the desire to fight the tyranny spreading across Europe. Others left Ireland to work in British war industries, where their labor kept factories humming and supply lines alive. At home, neutrality did not mean idleness: Irish coastal watchers scanned the Atlantic for U-boats, emergency services responded to domestic bombings in Dublin and Belfast, and rationing reshaped daily life. Irish doctors, nurses, engineers, and merchant mariners also played critical roles – many at great personal risk. Though unofficial and often unacknowledged for years, the contribution of ordinary Irish citizens to the war effort remains one of the most complex and remarkable chapters of Ireland's twentieth century story.

On the Emerald Isle, The Emergency reshaped daily life. Turf fires warmed homes because coal imports dried up. Tea, gasoline, and flour were rationed. Bicycles became family treasure. Rural families whispered at night about Luftwaffe planes straying over Irish skies, about the bodies of sailors washing ashore from torpedoed ships in the Atlantic, about Allied servicemen quietly "escaped" with a wink.

By 1945 the war was over, but Ireland emerged from it isolated and economically battered. Dublin was a capital of dim lights and thin wallets. Emigration returned with a vengeance – ships to Liverpool and trains to Cobh filled with young men and women fleeing poverty for factory work in England or dreams of New York. The diminished population shrank again. Rural parishes saw whole generations vanish across the sea.

Yet beneath this outward stagnation, Ireland was fastidiously reinventing itself. In 1948, a new inter-party government surprised even its members by doing what had been unthinkable for decades: it declared Ireland a *republic*. The Republic of Ireland Act severed the last constitutional link with the British Crown and took effect on Easter Monday, 1949 – the same memorialized date on which the Easter Rising had proclaimed independence thirty-three years earlier. London responded by doubling down on Northern Ireland's position within the United Kingdom and fortifying the border that had carved the island in two since 1921.

The 1950s brought a mix of gloom and grit – of poverty and progress. Economically, the country struggled. Protectionist policies kept foreign goods and foreign investment out, choking growth. At the same time, rural electrification began to spread, stringing wires over bog and mountain, lighting parish halls and farm kitchens for the first time. The Vatican's influence soared. The Irish political class seemed frozen between the ideals of 1916 and the realities of modern Europe.

And still, the people pushed forward. Writers like Brendan Behan and Flann O'Brien brought dark humor and sharp rebellion to Irish literature. In sports, the nation roared over Christy Ring on the hurling field (and if you haven't seen the Irish sport of hurling, you've been missing quite a spectacle). New political voices began to question whether isolation could ever bring prosperity.

By the 1960s, Ireland remained modest, rural, and conservative – a country of bicycles, church bells, and broad green fields extending to the Atlantic. It was also stronger, more self-defined, but more troubles were still in store in the decades to follow.

The Troubles

The Irish are known for having a way with words and one of Ireland's great understatements was a soft, almost polite euphemism for a conflict that spanned three decades and claimed more than 3,500 lives. In Irish society, a "trouble" might mean a sick calf, a rowdy cousin, or a bit of bad weather; yet by the late twentieth century, the word had come to signify bombings in city centers, assassinations on quiet roads, riots, internment, hunger strikes, and the grinding tension of a society split along political, national, and religious lines. To call such a period merely "troubled" was not denial but a cultural instinct: to wrap horror in modest language, to speak of catastrophe as though it were a bothersome misfortune rather than a bloody national wound. In that understatement lies a distinctly Irish mixture of irony, stoicism, and sorrow – an acknowledgment that the reality was too large, too painful, too *impolite*, to name without softening the blow.

The Troubles arrived not as a thunderclap but as a slow-rolling storm, thickening over Northern Ireland in the late 1960s as civil-rights marches met police batons, and politics hardened into fear. The border counties, where Catholic farms backed up against Protestant towns, felt the tension first. In places like Fermanagh, Tyrone, and South Armagh, families with names that had lived there for centuries – O'Neill, Gallagher, Maguire, McGrath –

found their quiet rural rhythms replaced by nightly patrols, checkpoints, and the unsettling hum of helicopters overhead. Armored cars patrolled the streets of Belfast.

Among the affected were the McGraths, a family name scattered widely across Ulster – an ancient Gaelic clan trapped in yet another new conflict. Some wore police uniforms; others attended civil-rights marches; still others tried only to keep their heads down. Yet history rarely permits neutrality for long.

In Belfast, there was yet another a young man named Patrick McGrath, a Catholic and one of several McGraths killed during the early 1970s. This Patrick became one of the first victims of sectarian gunfire in the city's rising chaos. His death, like so many in those years, blended tragedy with anonymity: another name listed in the newspaper, a funeral crowded into a terraced street, a family in mourning. He wasn't famous, but his story mirrored thousands of Irish who would die after him in the battle for a unified island.

Meanwhile, in County Armagh, a different McGrath confronted the storm from the opposite side. Constable Thomas McGrath of the RUC (Royal Ulster Constabulary) served during the fiercest years of bombings and ambushes, a Catholic officer in a force viewed by many nationalists as being aligned with the enemy. RUC Catholics were rare, and they lived with suspicion from both communities – yet some, like McGrath, persisted in the belief that policing could be a shield rather than a weapon. His service, recorded in routine reports rather than headlines, demonstrated another, quieter form of courage.

The Troubles intensified through the 1970s: internment without trial, Bloody Sunday, tit-for-tat killings by the IRA, the UVF, and the UDA; bombs in Derry, Belfast, London, Birmingham. Families watched more sons emigrate to escape the violence, join the British Army, or drift toward the paramilitaries that offered a sense of nationalist purpose. A few McGraths appear in court documents or prison rolls – low-level IRA couriers, men charged with possession of explosives, or youths caught transporting weapons. There were McGraths on both sides of the conflict.

By the 1980s and 1990s, when hunger strikes, political negotiations, and back-channel diplomacy slowly reshaped the terrain, the McGraths remained witnesses more often than protagonists. They manned shops in Derry, taught school in Tyrone, guarded checkpoints in Newry, and buried cousins caught in crossfire. The Good Friday Agreement in 1998 ended the hostilities on paper, but for many McGrath families – as for Northern Ireland itself – the peace felt fragile, like a truce built on an unstable pile of bones and old resentments.

For decades, Ireland's north and south had been weighed down by division, fear, and violence. Streets once alive with music and laughter were scarred by bombings, shootings, and the bitter mistrust between communities. Yet, even in the darkest years, hope endured: ordinary people who believed that dialogue, compromise, and courage could triumph over hatred kept working for peace and reconciliation. Their efforts bore fruit. Hard borders became bridges, checkpoints were replaced with "Welcome" signs (letting motorists know that speed limits were now in miles instead of kilometers per hour or vice versa) and towns that had known fear embraced reconciliation. Across Ireland, investment, tourism, and education grew. Today, descendants of historic McGrath families are part of an Irish renaissance: entrepreneurs like Eoin McGrath, helping revive local industries in Clare; artists such as Siobhán McGrath, bringing traditional Irish music to international stages; and civic leaders across Dublin and Belfast who dedicate themselves to community building and reconciliation.

Ireland stands as a testament to the power of endurance and collaboration. Cities hum with innovation, rural villages thrive with culture and agriculture, and communities remember the past while looking forward. Irish culture and even the Irish Gaelic language made a comeback during an era of peace for the island.

The McGraths, like so many families, continue to contribute to this renaissance, proving that even after centuries of struggle, the island's beautiful spirit can shine brightly. The pubs are filled with laughter and music. Local artists sell their works and paint commemorative murals. A thriving tourism industry provided a great boost to the economy, enabling new businesses to spring up and compete on the global stage. Across the isle, McGraths now own companies in numerous industries, including refrigeration and air conditioning; glass and ceramics; construction and building materials; real estate; transportation; beauty; and more. In America, the businesses now owned by McGraths are too numerous to list, but McGrath RentCorp, and McGrath Properties are examples of tremendous success for the clan across the pond.

With history as a guide, we can guess new challenges will inevitably present themselves, but for now, circumstances are better than they had been for a long, long, long, long time.

The Bardic Tradition Continues

After a thousand years of turmoil and tumult, the tradition of the ancient Clann Chraith Bardic School lives on. There are a plethora of McGraths noted for their work in art, music, poetry, literature and media. Of course, not everyone with the name is so inclined and McGraths can be found in every conceivable profession and position, from tradesmen, drivers, restaurateurs and soldiers to CEOs. But, the bardic tradition remains strong with us McGraths. I was drawn to writing and music long before I knew it was a clan legacy!

As I put the finishing touches on this book, an absolute genius writer who shares a name with me has just passed away. Dan McGrath (July 20, 1964 – November 14, 2025) was a writer and producer on the legendary comedy series The Simpsons for decades.

American poets like Campbell McGrath and Thomas McGrath have also carried the McGrath legacy into a contemporary voice. Campbell's sweeping long-form poems chronicle the heartbeat of modern America, while Thomas's politically charged works echo the socially conscious bardic call to witness and critique the world. Irish novelist Eamonn McGrath carried the storytelling tradition into fiction, his novels weaving memory, identity, and post-war Ireland into rich narrative tapestries.

Author MJ McGrath's work draws on Irish mythology, modernism, and romantic themes.

The tradition is not limited to the written word. Tom McGrath, a Scottish-Irish poet and musician, infused the countercultural 1960s with spoken word, jazz, and defiant experimentation, a modern echo of the itinerant bard performing in town squares and castles centuries before.

Mark McGrath and Catherine McGrath carry the musical torch. Mark is famous as the lead singer of American band Sugar Ray while Catherine is a rising star as a Northern Ireland pop-country music singer-songwriter.

Raymond McGrath, the architect and printmaker, brought imagination and Irish design to life, blending story and structure much like a bard inscribing tales into stone or parchment.

Across Canada, Wendy McGrath keeps the bardic tradition alive through spoken word and literary collaboration, while in television, Bob McGrath's decades of performances on Sesame Street carried storytelling to millions of young viewers, merging education with narrative in a way that harks back to the bardic purpose: to teach, to entertain, and to preserve the spirit of the people.

There are so many more – a whole book could be written just on the creative work of people bearing the McGrath name. Through these modern McGraths, the bardic tradition lives on. Transformed, modernized, perhaps, but unmistakable. Poetry, music, storytelling, history and artistry all converge, proving that the McGraths remain, centuries later, the heirs of Ireland's bardic soul.

Chieftains

A list of known historical Clan McGrath chieftains and the year they assumed the role.

Year	Chieftain Name
- 1290	Giolla Mac Craith
1290	Nicholas, son of Giolla Mac Craith
1340	Muiris, son of Nicholas Mac Craith
1384	Mark, son of Muiris Mac Craith
1423	Seán Mor, son of Muiris Mac Craith
1435	Matthew, brother of Seán Mor Mac Craith
1440	Seán Bui, son of Seán Mor Mac Craith
1469	Diarmuid, son of Mark, son of Muiris
1491	Rory, son of Diarmuid
1528	Torlough, son of Andrew Mac Craith
1549	"The Mac Craith," first name unknown
1562	Donncha, father of Miler McGrath
1596	James, son of Archbishop Miler McGrath
1641	Turlogh, son of James McGrath
1691	Brian, son of Turlogh McGrath
unknown	Seamus Og, son of Turlogh McGrath
unknown	Reamonn, son of Seamus Og

The Clan, Today

There now exist two distinct septs of Clan McGrath: The McGraths of Ulster and the McGraths of Thomond (consisting of McGraths from Waterford and Tipperary). Each has it's own leadership. The term "chieftain" is no longer used by either sept, preferring now the Irish term *Ceann Fine,* which means "Head of the family." Each sept has it's own Ceann Fine. For the Thomond McGrath's, that was Joanne Hickey as of this writing in 2025. The Ulster chief was Seán Alexander McGrath.

The division between the septs has been bridged. They are now united by the Clan McGrath Society, which in turn has it's own *Taoiseach* (chief). As of 2025, The Clan McGrath Society's chief was Scott McGraw (check Chapter 1, Page 7 "All one Family," if you need a reminder that McGraws are McGraths, too!)

These various clan chiefs are elected from members of the clan and they, along with their clan councils plan and execute various clan gatherings.

As a constitutional republic, Ireland today firmly rejects the creation or recognition of noble titles. The *Bunreacht na hÉireann* (the Irish Constitution) dictates that the State *"shall not confer any title of nobility"*, and further prohibits citizens from accepting foreign titles without government permission. As a result, traditional Gaelic titles such as "Chief of the Name," *Tánaiste*, or

Chieftain have no legal authority or status in the Republic of Ireland.

From the 1940s until 2003, the Irish government, through the Chief Herald of Ireland, offered *courtesy recognition* of clan chiefs. These chiefs, usually the senior descendants of historic Gaelic ruling families, were styled as "Chiefs of the Name."

In 2003, the practice ended after legal concerns were raised—specifically, the question of whether acknowledging chiefs violated the constitutional prohibition on noble titles. Even though the recognition was symbolic, the Attorney General advised ceasing the practice. Since then, the Irish State no longer certifies or acknowledges clan chiefs in any official capacity.

Keeping track of clan chiefs has thus become a strictly family matter, but an organization called Clans of Ireland (*Finte na hÉireann* in Irish) now maintains a register of Irish clans and their chieftains. Though not an official government organization, they have boasted as their patron, the president of Ireland.

Every two years, the Clan McGrath Society organizes a gathering that tours various castles and properties historically associated with the McGraths.

One need not be a resident of Ireland to join the Clan McGrath society. It is an international organization and registration is FREE!

Check them out at their website: https://clanmcgrath.org/

About the Author

Dan McGrath was born in Minneapolis, where he still lives and pursues creative hobbies like painting, writing and music production. He became a licensed pilot in 2023.

He has extensive experience working in and around politics and government. He has served as executive director, president and communications director for non-profit organizations, a campaign manager for candidates, chairman of a ballot committee and a registered lobbyist. He has also launched several successful lawsuits against government entities and won cases in both the Minnesota and United States Supreme Courts.

Dan has been featured in numerous national and local television and radio programs and newspapers.

Before getting roped into political work, Dan was an avid gamer, co-owner of a game and comic book shop called Red Dragon Hobby and the creator of the original 1997 role playing game, MagiQuest.

Learn more at DanMcGrath.net

Other Books by Dan McGrath

MagiQuest

What Everyone Should Know About the Government

The Adventures of Dan and Tina

The Voter Fraud Manual

The Storm Tower

UFO Farmers

9 7 9 8 9 8 7 6 1 6 9 4 9